A CENTURY OF COACHING ON EXMOOR

A CENTURY OF
COACHING ON EXMOOR

'Horner Woods for Tea'

MICHAEL HAWKINS
& ROGER GRIMLEY

EXMOOR BOOKS

First published in 1998 by Exmoor Books
Copyright © 1998 Michael Hawkins and Roger Grimley

ISBN 0 86183 450 X

British Library Cataloguing-in-Publication-Data
A CIP data for this book is available from the British Library

EXMOOR BOOKS
Dulverton, Somerset

Trade enquiries:
HALSGROVE
Halsgrove House
Lower Moor Way
Tiverton EX16 6SS
T: 01884 243242
F: 01884 243325
www.halsgrove.com

*Exmoor Books is a partnership between The Exmoor Press
and The Exmoor National Park Authority*

Printed and bound in Great Britain by
WBC Ltd, Bridgend

Dedicated to the memory of

William and Jack Hawkins

and all the other pioneer coach

operators in the Exmoor area.

Contents

Foreword

I have found Mr Hawkins' and Mr Grimley's book as entertaining as it is informative. Their extensive research into the changing modes of passenger transport in the Exmoor region from the fourteenth century to the present day not only provides facts about horse-drawn and, later, motorised carriages – routes, fares, conditions of travel and journey times – but it also tells of the growth of the tourist industry in Minehead and West Somerset, of the effect on this area of the two world wars and, of course, of the changes in the roads themselves.

We learn about many local characters and about the varied enterprises in addition to public transport with which some were involved. The authors mention several interesting facts of which I for one was previously ignorant, for example that in the early part of the last century Lynton maintained a local time which was twenty minutes behind that of London.

I am sure all readers will enjoy this book as much as I have, and I am delighted to have been invited to provide this Foreword.

Col. Sir Walter Luttrell, KCVO, MC

A very early view of The Parade side of the Feathers Hotel in Minehead with horses being put into the shafts of a coach. The name of the landlord, Thristle, is seen on the portico and this family was also involved in the coach trade, having an interest in the 'Red Deer' to and from Lynton. (ROH)

Authors' Preface

As a young man growing up in Minehead in the 1930s and 1940s the Scarlet Pimpernel was not for me the humble English wayside flower, nor the hero in Baroness Orczy's famous novel, but the huge gleaming red coaches of the family business that absorbed my father Bill and his brother Jack's working life.

It is only in recent years that I began to realise that whereas the part played by the bus and coach in the social history of the twentieth century is well documented, the major contribution that the touring coach played in what is now the leisure industry, and in particular in the development of Minehead and the other popular holiday resorts of Exmoor, was in danger of being overlooked. Yet at the peak period as many as 44 coaches were operated from Minehead and a staggering figure of over 80 vehicles from Ilfracombe on a daily basis. They arguably provided a major contribution not only to the economy of the area but also to the development of the resorts.

The problem in starting late to record the history of the industry is that many of the personalities involved have died. Fortunately help was at hand from the many people with memories of the time and also from those for whom transport history provides a passionate and highly specialised interest, some of whom have even saved and lovingly restored important coaches of the time, including some 'Scarlet Pimpernels'. This is my opportunity to thank all of those who gave us their help and support in preparing this book.

One of the foremost experts in the field of transport history in the Westcountry is Roger Grimley. It was a fortunate day for me when Roger agreed to collaborate in writing this history. Indeed without his detailed research into the history of horse-drawn coaches and the many motor proprietors operating at the time, this book could not have been written. I am truly grateful for his patient and painstaking help throughout its preparation.

I am sometimes asked to describe my lasting impression of the coach business in Minehead at the peak of its popularity in the late 1940s and 1950s. I could refer to the undoubted elegance of the vehicles and the immaculate condition in which they were maintained, or the holiday atmosphere in a town catering for a type of family holiday long since gone. However, my most vivid recollection centres on the daily scene at 9.30am, repeated at 2.30pm, when numerous coaches of all colours, styles and makes dominated the centre of Minehead as hundreds of eager holidaymakers boarded to set off to the many destinations. Then, exactly at departure time, the drivers of the Leylands, Daimlers, Bedfords and many other makes would climb into their seats, start the engines, and move off, the scores of vehicles appearing to totally monopolise the main roads. After a few minutes they had disappeared and the town centre reverted to its normal business.

Paradoxically much of my professional life was spent in controlling and coping with the relentless growth of traffic. During my 17 years as County Engineer and Planning Officer of Devon, this included, as fate dictated, curtailing the intrusion of coaches into the two National Parks. If my father and his brother ever thought my role in restricting the coach on Exmoor and Dartmoor was even remotely disloyal to the family tradition, they were kind enough not to say so.

This history of 100 years of coaching between the mid-nineteenth and mid-twentieth century is therefore a fitting opportunity to pay a tribute to all those pioneers who played a part in the coach business throughout that period to the lasting benefit of the area.

Michael Hawkins, OBE

Exmoor has a magical quality. The beauty of the scenery, the wildlife and the legends make it a very special and unique place for the country-lover. It is also very special for the transport historian.

As a child growing up in rural Devon I loved the countryside and listened to the stories of life in days gone by. I heard firsthand accounts from older people and saw for myself how much life had changed as a result of improved communications. My family was involved in transport and I got to know every part of the Westcountry. Gradually I began to piece together the development of transport and how it affected life in the rural areas.

Good communications were late coming to Exmoor and over thirty years elapsed from the time the railways reached Bridgwater until the first train arrived at Minehead. At Lynton the twentieth century was about to dawn when the narrow-gauge line from Barnstaple was opened.

The area is also unique in that the railways did not kill off the horse-drawn, four-in-hand coaches. At a time when coach routes were fast disappearing and the four-in-hand was seen as old-fashioned and romantic in other parts of the country, around Exmoor the railways acted as a catalyst and new coach routes opened up linking railheads with resorts.

The terrain of West Somerset and North Devon presented the coach operators with considerable problems. Dragging a heavily laden coach up gradients of one in four, around hairpin bends on rough surfaces, was a challenge for man and beast; coming down was dangerous, with little in the way of braking to help horses straining to hold back the loaded vehicle. Exmoor had some of the most difficult coach routes in the country.

As motor traction developed Exmoor was again later than other areas in embracing the new mode of transport. Local roads were generally considered too dangerous for the early motors and it was not until the 1920s that the internal-combustion engine served the needs of local people and visitors to the area to any great extent. Then rapid improvements in vehicle design and changing social habits altered the area for ever and transport played a key role in the development of the district.

But transport is a means, not an end. It enables people to travel for a purpose and it is the people that give 'life' to the story. The proprietors of the horse drawn and motor vehicles were enterprising and needed both determination and ingenuity in large measure if they were to succeed. Their drivers were independent and self-reliant characters who ensured the safety of the passengers and acted as guide. They 'told the tale' and could turn an ordinary journey into an unforgettable experience. The early passengers, who were generally well-to-do, needed a spirit of adventure and a willingness to endure considerable discomfort. Then buses and coaches developed to become part of everyday life, patronised by the majority of the population until the advent of mass ownership of private cars from the 1960s.

During my working life, which was largely in agriculture but always with some involvement with transport, I realised that the memories of coaching and early motor bus operation were being lost for ever. I started to record personal recollections and records of those times and over the years realised that the reason why people travelled is an integral part of the story.

As one who appreciates beautiful country and as a historian I find Exmoor fascinating. It has been a pleasure to work with Michael Hawkins and the story we tell is about the everyday life of Exmoor people and of those who over the years have come to experience the magic of this wonderful part of the Westcountry. Our story is about people and about a place.

Roger Grimley

The remarkable feat of an ex-First World War RAF reconditioned vehicle negotiating Porlock Hill with a full load of passengers and luggage on a daily basis prompted the manufacturers, Leyland Motors, proudly to advertise its performance in a 1921 edition of Motor Transport. The conductor is ready to jump off the platform and place a chock under the wheel if the engine stalls. (PM)

Leyland

By Royal Appointment

CLIMBING PORLOCK
DAILY.

HERE IS POSITIVE PROOF OF THE STAYING POWER OF THE LEYLAND R.A.F. RECONDITIONED VEHICLE.

One of the most difficult hills in England negotiated daily by a Leyland Single-decker WITH FULL LOAD AND LUGGAGE.

A motor service has been inaugurated between Minehead and Lynmouth. This photo illustrates a Leyland R.A.F. Reconditioned machine negotiating the stiffest hairpin corner —the gradient of which varies between 3 and 5 to 1.

ad Office & Works: ᵛLAND, LANCS.

London Office and Overseas Dept.:
47, New Kent Road, S.E.1.

Kindly mention "Motor Transport" when replying to this advertisement.

Acknowledgements

The authors express their gratitude to the many people who have helped with information, recollections or by allowing the use of their photographs. The latter have been denoted by initials, as shown below, and included in the captions of illustrations.

Thanks to Allerford Rural Life Museum (AM), Peter Anderson (PA), K. Astell (KA), Graham Batten, Beaford Archive (BA), Pauline Bennett, Mrs C. Boyles, Geoff Bruce, George Burnell, Dennis Corner, Bob Crawley (CPC), Alan B. Cross (ABC), Stephen Dear, Doris Derrick, Dick Dibble (RD), Chris Dyer (CD), Frances Edbrooke, Mr and Mrs A. Ell, Exmoor National Park Authority, Exmoor Photographic Archive (EPA), Exmoor Society, Doris Fischer, Richard Ford, Mrs P. Gillard, R.O. Hancock (ROH), Bessie Hawkins, Robin and Maureen Hawkins, Richard Hobbs (RH), Malcolm Johnson, Donald Jones, the late Roy Lee (RL), Roger Langrish, Roy Marshall (RM), John Newton, North Devon Journal/ Herald, Dick Okill (RO), Omnibus Society (OS), John Pedder, Philip Platt, PSV Circle, Derek Poole, Porlock Museum (PM), Royal Automobile Club, Malcolm Scott (MS), Colin Shears (CS), Somerset County Council (SCC), Desmond Southgate, Vera Sparkes, Shirley and Roger Spencer (SS), Kath Staddon (KS), Terry Venner, West Somerset Free Press, Sidney Whitehead (SW) and to the many others who have helped with snippets of information that have added to the story. Illustrations marked (RG), (MH) and (PC) are from the authors' collections, PC denoting 'postcard'. The source of some views is unknown so these cannot be acknowledged.

Thanks to Judy Hawkins and Barbara Grimley for their help and and for being so patient and understanding while we have been working on this book.

With historical research there are, at times, uncertainties but we have endeavoured to be as accurate as possible. If there are any discrepancies they are the fault of the authors, who can only apologise. If anyone can add to or correct the record we would be delighted to hear from them.

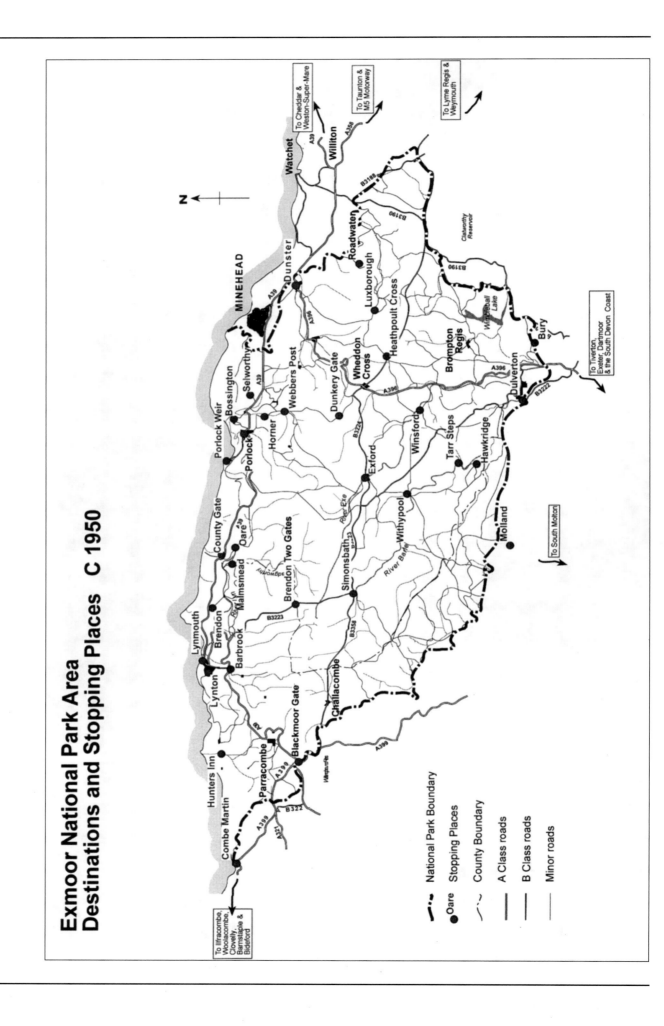

Exmoor National Park Area
Destinations and Stopping Places   C 1950

Part One
SETTING THE SCENE

Introduction

To look round the next bend or to see what is on the far side of the hill has been man's inherent desire from time immemorial.

By the fourteenth century there was a network of lanes linking the towns, villages, hamlets and farmsteads of England, some having their origins in the trackways along the high ridges traversed by early man. However, the state of the Westcountry roads in the Middle Ages – rough and unpleasant, painful for man and horse – did little to encourage anything other than essential journeys. At the relatively slow speed possible, travel between Exmoor and London took days. The cost of horses, food and accommodation en route was high and travel was only for the well-to-do. For the vast majority there was no option but to remain within walking distance of their home.

By the late eighteenth century those with a desire to travel, and the means to pay for it, went abroad. When the Napoleonic Wars prevented them from doing so, they were forced to explore their own country and the scenic beauties of Exmoor were among the discoveries they made.

Numbers were initially restricted by the difficulties of travelling by land in an area which was a wilderness, and by the risk of storm and tempest involved in sea journeys. But among the early visitors were poets who helped to make more widely known the beauty, charm and attraction of the area and increasing numbers came over the packhorse tracks to see what became known as 'The English Switzerland'.

To ease their passage the roads were improved and special accommodation arranged for the visitors. The fishing villages of Lynton, Lynmouth and Minehead developed into resorts and gradually tourism provided income for a growing proportion of the population. The hunting, shooting and fishing opportunities attracted others and the Dulverton area became a centre for sportsmen. The first travellers by land came in their private coaches and the stage- and mail-coach services that crisscrossed most of England at first left Exmoor largely untouched.

The Victorian era witnessed the greatest social revolution that this country has ever seen. If the foundation for that giant social and economic leap was based on the steam engine it would be the internal-combustion engine that provided the momentum to carry the progress forward into the twentieth century. Very few parts of the country remained untouched and West Somerset and North Devon were no exception, albeit somewhat delayed. Exmoor and its communities were destined to be transformed from an inaccessible wilderness and quiet, largely self-sufficient towns and villages into the popular area enjoyed by millions that it is today.

Many factors contributed to this transition but there was one major industry that would play an important role through the entire period and without which the change in the local economy could never have been achieved. This was, of course, the coaching industry, using first the four-in-hand and stagecoach, and later the motor coach.

The development of railways brought dramatic changes to travel, trans-forming the pace of life. As the lines were extended across England so the coach services withered and died. However, in West Somerset the opposite was the case. The railways were late arriving. Although Bridgwater was reached in 1841, it was over thirty years before a line was constructed to Minehead and the century was almost over before the first train arrived at Lynton from Barnstaple. The railways never penetrated beyond the periphery of Exmoor.

For much of the second half of the nineteenth century travellers could enjoy a train journey as far as Taunton, Dulverton, Williton (later Minehead) or Barnstaple but then had to resort to road transport to reach the attractions of Exmoor. To meet the needs of the increased numbers of visitors, coach services were started, linking railhead with resort. While in most of the country the old stagecoach was being remembered as a relic of the past, around Minehead, Lynton and Lynmouth horse-drawn coach services were just reaching their peak.

The limited carrying capacity, together with fares affordable only by the affluent minority, meant that the coaches did not provide mass transportation. The single fare between Minehead and Lynmouth (about six shillings and sixpence) was roughly the same as a farm worker in the South West might earn in a week, but it was difficult for the coach proprietor to achieve profitability as the hilly roads were a severe test for the horses and frequent changes were necessary. Large numbers of animals had to be kept along the route and, even so, the average speed on the Lynton and Minehead road was only about 5 miles an hour compared to the normal 10 mph for a four-in-hand coach elsewhere. Traffic was seasonal and the cost of food, stabling and staff had to be reclaimed over a comparatively short season.

As the twentieth century dawned the internal-combustion engine provided a new mode of transport but it made a faltering start and did not have the same impact as the railways. Even as motors gained more widespread acceptance in much of the country the geography of Exmoor prevented their exploitation until there had been considerable advances in engine and braking design. Once again West Somerset and North Devon developed more slowly than the rest of the country and horse traction continued to dominate locally. It was not until the 1920s that motor vehicles had developed sufficiently to be considered safe enough to be used fully on Exmoor roads.

This coincided with a time of high expectation after the end of the Great War. The general population, weary of deprivation and death, wanted nothing more than to exercise their new-found freedom to travel and enjoy themselves. Returning servicemen, who had learned to drive and maintain motors during their war service, invested their gratuity and savings in one or more of the many surplus military vehicles then available. The motor bus and charabanc business grew rapidly and the early open bodied solid tyred vehicles were soon superseded by streamlined coaches with comfort equal to a private car. Travel was no longer the preserve of the wealthy, the mass of the population were now able to see more of the world.

The advent of the motor charabanc (or char-a-banc, from the French *char-à-bancs*, meaning carriage with benches) was not welcomed by everyone. At times strenuous efforts were made to restrict or prohibit heavy traffic on country roads. When such regulations were being considered in Devon in 1923 it was stated at the Ministry of Transport public inquiry that what largely underlay the application was undoubtedly the motor charabanc. The local press reflected 'the poetic senses of county folk did not appreciate the class of vehicle. They did not consider the loud horn was beautiful but regarded it as a most infernal din. They looked on the motor coach as a perfect pest and an absolute nuisance.'

However, public transport continued to grow and writing about how to attract passengers to bus and coach services, W.J. Crosland Taylor, a well-known transport manager of the time, said:

> We in the road transport business must so arrange our affairs that we can pick out all the people who find themselves in the wrong place and move them as quickly and as cheaply as possible to the right place; having done that, we must persuade them that where they came from was the right place after all, and it would be best to go back there – indeed we will help them to do this by reducing the price of the return journey, the return ticket having been invented for that very purpose. We have not only to do that, but to help us on a bit we must find fresh means to persuade a lot of people who are really quite all right where they are, that it would be ever so much better if they went somewhere else, and no doubt returned in due course.

Over the following four or five decades motor buses and coaches provided the principal means by which the greater part of the population explored the countryside and visited other towns and cities. Motor transport was cheaper to provide and often more convenient than the railways, as witnessed by the demise in 1935 of the narrow-gauge Lynton and Barnstaple Railway, largely the victim of road competition. It was the 'golden age' of the bus and coach.

The two world wars dramatically changed social habits and paid annual holidays for working people transformed travel patterns. A wider section of the population was now able to come to Minehead, which changed from a rather select town on the coast catering for those seeking the sport and quiet recreation afforded by the nearby moor to a family holiday resort. The rod and the artist's palette gave way to the bucket and spade.

Exmoor became accessible and every day during the summer season literally hundreds of coaches from resorts far and near carried holidaymakers to the beauty spots and places of interest on and around the moor. From Minehead alone over forty motor coaches vied for the custom of those visitors seeking a trip out.

Even quiet little Dulverton, tucked away on the southern edges of Exmoor away from the coast, did not entirely escape the hordes. It became a popular stop on charabanc trips across Exmoor but before their arrival and after their departure it resumed its sleepy quiet. Out at Brushford, adjacent to Dulverton station, the sportsmen continued to patronise the Carnarvon Arms Hotel.

Following the restraint and austerity of the Second World War, there was an unprecedented boom in the use of public transport, but ominous signs of change were apparent. Aspirations were now higher and the ambition to have 'a little car of our own' was realised in increasing numbers. Public transport lost traffic as people chose, and could afford, to have personal transport. Bus and train services were drastically reduced and within a century of its opening the branch line between Taunton and Minehead was closed. But by then the die was cast. The future of Exmoor as a holiday destination had been established and there was no going back.

In a period spanning two centuries West Somerset and North Devon had changed from being remote and inaccessible into a popular area struggling to cope with the volume of visitors. Although the coach industry played a significant part in the development, this has never been fully recognised in the many publications written about the time. This book attempts to rectify this.

Tracks, Turnpikes and Gradients

Roads form an important part of our history and the roadsides abound with features that chronicle the development of the country through the ages. There are the ridgeways, the old Roman roads and the former turnpikes, of which numerous tollhouses are distinctive reminders. The days of packhorse and stagecoach are brought to mind by packhorse bridges, milestones, drinking troughs, markers and even notices threatening transportation for those found tampering with bridges. Fascinating as is the history of the highways and byways, it is beyond the scope of this book; however, it is important to appreciate their significance in the story of the Westcountry coach trade.

The importance of the legacy of a good road network left by the Romans was lost on our ancestors, who allowed what roads there were to fall into disrepair. Eventually it fell to private enterprise to find the answer through the Turnpike Trusts, the first of which was established in 1706. As with the railways, turnpikes were slow to arrive in West Somerset and it was not until 1765 that the Minehead turnpike legislation was approved. This set in place what is now the A39 towards Bridgwater and the A396 towards Bampton.

Some farmers raised objections to the turnpikes that strained credulity. For example, it was alleged that the raising and draining of the roads did away with

Toll houses and tollkeeper's cottages were an essential feature of the turnpike era. Many still survive and this one, on the A396 road approaching Dunster, is less readily recognised than many. This view, taken in the 1930s, shows a Western National Dennis bus at the Forester's Arms terminus. (PC)

the pools of water and soft moist surface that was necessary for preserving the hoofs of horses, and enabled them to drink and refresh themselves on their journeys. One old coachman would not use the new roads, but stuck to the old wagon tracks. His father had driven on the slush before him and he would stick to it until death. Another waggoner thought that the roads had but one purpose: horses and waggons; he required but a width of 5 feet in the road, and all the rest might go to the devil. He thought the gentry should stay at home and not run gossiping up and down the country.

Although immensely unpopular, the turnpikes provided the first real network of good-quality roads and transformed the quality and speed of coach travel. The advent of the railways expedited the demise of the Turnpike Trusts and by 1896 they had all but ceased to exist, leaving behind a network of 20,000 miles of roads.

As the Turnpike Trusts gave up, responsibilty for the roads fell back on the parishes and what maintenance there was often amounted to throwing stones on to the surface and leaving the traffic to work it in. Except for the roads serving the railway stations and market towns, road traffic became mainly local. By the 1890s the British highways were in a bad way, forgotten by Parliament, neglected by the parishes.

The story of the modern road really began with the Local Government Act of 1888, which established the County Councils. The former turnpikes became the basis of the national major road network in the first half of the twentieth century and were 'tarmacked' by the 1920s. The many hundreds of miles of unclassified by-roads for which North Devon and West Somerset is renowned were not surface-dressed until as late as the 1930s.

There is another type of road: that based on the ancient ridgeways. Prehistoric man travelled on high ground above the forests and around the sources of streams and rivers safe from predatory animals. He tended to follow familiar routes and in so doing created a national network of ridgeways that is still in use today.

Exmoor is laced with ridgeways, their importance to prehistoric man being recorded by the barrows and stone markers to be found at intervals along the way. Many form the basis of the routes today. On Exmoor, the ridgeway running close to the A39 between Lynmouth and Porlock was the most noteworthy. East from Porlock the way continued, climbing Bossington Hill, then along the ridge of North Hill past Selworthy Beacon to descend into Minehead via Holloway Street. This section defeated even the most determined road-builder, but not so Porlock Hill.

The hill between Porlock village and Exmoor has always presented a challenge for horse-drawn and motor vehicles. Its notoriety arises not only from the length of its very steep gradient but from the added surprise of a one-in-four hairpin bend at its mid-point. The road between Countisbury and Lynmouth is equally daunting and although the two hills are recognised throughout the land, even today they come as a surprise to motorists who are more used to geometrically designed highways with gentle gradients.

For the timid, or those without confidence in the ability of their vehicle to make it to the top or bottom of Porlock Hill, there is the alternative of the Toll Road. Some four and a half miles in length, it has a much easier gradient and starts near the Ship Inn at Porlock, emerging at Pittcombe Cross. Built by the lord of the manor, Mr Blathwayte, in about 1840, surprisingly it was first constructed as a scenic route, not as an alternative to Porlock Hill.

For the local coach companies, horse and motor, both Porlock and Countisbury Hills were part of everyday life. Horse-drawn vehicles coped by adding an extra pair of horses for the climb, removing some luggage and asking some passengers to walk. Motors were chosen with engines and gears capable of tackling the hills, if not in their stride at least with laboured ease.

A graphic description of what conditions were like in the early part of the twentieth century is given by John Presland in his book *Lynton and Lynmouth*. He tells us:

Porlock Hill, with its hairpin bends and a gradient of one in four, is nationally notorious. In the early days of motoring postcard producers anxious to heighten the drama of vehicles tackling the gradients were not above 'doctoring' views but this convoy of early charabancs descending seems genuine. (PC)

Countisbury Hill. Few roads in the United Kingdom are as challenging or the views so spectacular. While the gradients match those of Porlock Hill, the latter receives more publicity. (PC)

If you take the carriage (in which case you will walk the greater part of the way!) you will start from Lynmouth and ascend the steep hill that leads right up the cliff at Countisbury Foreland. I should have said the steepest two miles of carriage road in England had I not also climbed Porlock Hill. ... The surface of the road is loose and scored by winter rains and on a windy day the dust comes swirling down like a miniature sandstorm. I have, indeed, even seen a car obliged to draw up and let the blinding red swirl go by.

Of Porlock Hill he says:

The road that leads from Exmoor down to Porlock is incredibly steep, the steepest coach road in England. It twists dangerously in sharp right-angle turns, the surface is loose and stony, worn by the dragging brakes and scouring of winter rains, and on a summer afternoon it is so hot, so dusty and glaring, and so steep, that it seems impossible for man or beast to climb'.

Two firsthand accounts of this period which appeared in the Exmoor Society publication 'The Exmoor Review' also give a flavour of ascending the hill. Patricia Powell recalls:

Our favourite driver was a Mr Staddon. The brake started outside his office in The Avenue, Minehead. Before the ascent of Porlock Hill the brake stopped at the Ship Inn at Porlock and additional horses harnessed. Adults walked up the hill and only the infirm and children rode.

Sidney Whitehead describes going up Porlock Hill at the end of the Great War:

The little slip road was not there then and all the traffic, up and down, had to go round the hairpin bend. I can just remember the passengers' screams when the bus lurched and seemed nearly to turn over. Of course it was solid tyres then and I believe the bus had an open platform at the back. We had a large hamper for our clothes and this was taken off the roof and left by the roadside near the (Porlock) Church. My mother was a bit reluctant but was told 'That's alright m'dear, the carter will bring it up later.'

The coach journey from Porlock up the hill was described in these words:

A phenomenal rise is made. To ascend just over a thousand feet in a little under a mile is, everyone will admit, a hill which is rarely met with in Europe, yet such we have just experienced and our six horses have had to work hard to haul the coach to the top.

Yet if going up was a challenge, descending was equally dangerous. It was Pickwick's Weller who shrewdly observed: 'Coaches is like guns – they requires to be loaded with wery great care afore they go off.' This was certainly true, for it was necessary not only to balance the load on the coach but also the 'wheelers', the two horses nearest the coach, had to be carefully paired for equal stride.
A local guide struck a very cautious note in the early days of motors:

The hill into Porlock deserves treating with considerable respect, the Ordnance Map allows it no fewer than four of those hated little broad arrows which mark an exceptionally tough gradient. A private road of gentler pitch goes off to the left just after Oare Post, and the wise motorist will regard the shilling toll charged as a kind of life and car insurance combined. Even on this way there is one hairpin bend needing care.

"LORNA DOONE COACH" DESCENDING PORLOCK HILL
GRADIENT 8¼ INCHES IN 2½ FEET.

'Lorna Doone' coach descending Porlock Hill, the passengers perched high above the road. The expression 'dropping off to sleep' is said to come from dozing passengers falling off the coach! A skid attached to the rear wheel is the only form of braking assistance for the horses and wheel marks can be seen in the loose road surface. Going up the hill was slow and difficult; coming down was dangerous. (PC)

An early motorist was Mrs Rodolph Stawell and in her *Motor Tours of the Westcountry* she notes:

Porlock Hill is a word of dread significance to those who are interested in the roads of England. A precipitous hill nearly three miles long, with the surface of sand and stone and several sharp corners – such is the vision that this name evokes.

Before setting out for the drive to Minehead, she continues:

From Lynton we look over the roofs of Lynmouth to Countisbury Hill and the red road that climbs it – apparently quite perpendicularly. Into the mind there steals a hope that this is not our road. But it is.

Porlock Hill was said to be 'a proverb for steepness in the Westcountry' but further west there were also gradients that challenged the traveller, as Mrs Stawell notes:

The famous hill between Lynton and Lynmouth thoroughly deserves its reputation and, after personal experience, I strongly advise motorists to avoid it unless they have absolute confidence in the staunchness of their car, the power of the brakes and the scope of their steering locks. Its difficulty lies not in its gradient – though at one point that is steeper than 1 in 4 – but in the extremely acute angle that occurs at the steepest point and makes it impossible, if there should chance be so much as a wheelbarrow by the wayside, for a car of any size to turn without passing. An added difficulty is the looseness of the soil, for the constant use of drags has ploughed it into a mass of stones and sand.

In later years things had improved somewhat and the surfaces at any rate were generally very good. But both Lynmouth and Castle Hills:

...are steep and the turn from one into the other is not one of the most enjoyable moments in the life of a driver whose car is towing a caravan.

On the Lynton to Ilfracombe road the sharp drop through the valley in which Parracombe village lies was another test:

Through Parracombe, where there are two hills of some renown, a descent and a climb. The inconvenience here is in the fact that the change

This steam lorry, owned by Kings of Bishops Lydeard, appears to be on the wrong side of the road. It is, in fact, reversing down Porlock Hill, the driver clearly putting safety first by using the additional braking afforded by the lower reverse gear. The RAC patrolman is guiding the lorry round the corner. The water tank beside the RAC box was a welcome sight to drivers whose radiators were boiling by the time they reached the top. (SW)

Reversing round the hairpin bend must have been difficult and the manoeuvre is anxiously watched by a bystander while a cyclist maintains his distance. (SW)

from the downwards to the upward gradient is in the middle of the village and a run is out of the question.

Others described the road surface here as 'wretched'.

One of the most comprehensive accounts of the history of Porlock Hill can be found in *Porlock in Those Days*, by Dennis Corner. The hill was for decades the extreme test for all types of vehicles and to this day remains a daunting experience for drivers not used to negotiating steep gradients on hairpin bends. The highway authority still retains the escape road for descending vehicles which get out of control, while an old-style A.A. Box (No. 137), now a listed building, stands at the top of the hill as a permanent reminder of those early days of motoring when cars with boiling radiators required attention at the top. Sadly the water container once situated there has long since disappeared. The R.A.C. Box (No. 460), located on the hill, has also been removed.

Even as late as the 1960s many a visitor came to grief on the hill, providing the local garages with a steady trade in towing and replacing burnt-out clutches. Today vehicles are of such high performance that Porlock and Countisbury Hills no longer instil in the driver the fear that they once did. Nevertheless, there are still occasional runaways, fortunately rarely too serious.

The hill had its place in local folklore and if anything was described as steep, the inevitable question would follow: 'As steep as Porlock Hill?'

If roads are part of the groundwork of civilisation, the bridge is frequently associated with the romance of the Queen's highway, with communities either linked by or growing up around them.

Exmoor has its share of historic bridges and while the early humble structures have long since disappeared, it has arguably the most splendid of all clapper bridges at Tarr Steps. There are also many fine packhorse bridges, such as those at Allerford and Horner with their characteristic low parapets to allow for the ponies.

At Dulverton and Lanacre there are excellent examples of masonry bridges equal to any to be found elsewhere, while at Lynmouth the replacement bridges to those swept away by the flood of 1952 utilised the concrete and steel of modern construction, albeit cleverly disguised.

The romance of countryside bridges is captured by this poem of the 1930s:

Song of Bridges

When ingenious Man
First thought of a plan
Of fashioning bridges the rivers to span
He did what he could,
Though they weren't very good –
He felled and he hewed and he built 'em of wood:
Springy new,
Swingy new,
Bridges of wood.

And village lovers often came
With clumsy knife and simple art,
Engraving each the other's name
Within an arrow-piercèd heart
(Lest any should their love forget)
Upon the oaken parapet.

Then up sprang a guild
Of stone-masons skilled,
And said 'Let us teach you to quarry and build;
For demolish you should
(Too long have they stood)
Your creaky old,
Leaky old,
Bridges of wood;
Storm-battered and blown,
They'll soon be overthrown;
If you want to be safe you must build 'em of stone –
Solid new,
Stolid new,
Bridges of stone.

And old men came to rest their bones
At evening when the work was done,
And lean upon the kindly stones
That all day long had drunk the sun,
And smoke their pipes, and talk, and sigh,
And hear the news from passers-by.

And now in our ears
Sound the warnings and jeers
Of architects learnèd and wise engineers:–
'Statistics have shown
That's the traffic's outgrown
Your bumpy old,
Humpy old,
Bridges of stone;
It's the Age of the Wheel,
And we earnestly feel
If you want to be safe you must build 'em of steel:
Dashing new,
Flashing new,
Bridges of steel.

But who will lean, I wonder, now,
Upon these rigid, frigid frames?
On this unyielding metal, how
Can rustic lovers carve their names?
Fie, fie! A truce to vain reproaches;
The world's made safe for motor coaches.

Jan Struther
In *Punch*, 1931

Part Two
THE ERA OF THE HORSE

Introduction

The evolution of transport was controlled by roads more than any other factor. In the early part of the eighteenth century they were still generally in a deplorable condition, but there had been some improvements. Heavy, lumbering wagons ran between London and the major towns in the Westcountry, carrying both goods and some passengers, and local carriers provided the link between the market towns and the surrounding countryside.

The horse-drawn coach was a major leap forward in the history of travel in England, even though in its early days it was not without its problems. Sydney Smith recorded that it took him nine hours to go by coach from Taunton to Bath and that on the journey he suffered 'between ten thousand and twelve thousand severe contusions'.

It was not until after the Turnpike Acts that regular, fast and efficient horse-drawn coach services were developed in the Westcountry. In the period that followed the coach played an important role in the development of Minehead and North Devon and when local roads too were improved Exmoor communities were linked with the national network, principally via Bridgwater and Exeter. The ancient ridgeway routes across Exmoor were destined to play an important part in the local travel pattern, most notably the spectacular route between Porlock and Lynton with its notorious gradients.

Stage- or flying coaches catered for needs at first but the introduction of fast mail coaches, provided by local contractors but carrying an armed, scarlet-coated Government servant as guard, brought new standards of speed, punctuality and safety. This attracted passengers from the stagecoaches, the proprietors of which were obliged to improve their service in order to compete for the favours of the travelling public; considerable rivalry was created.

By the early part of the nineteenth century Britain had a network of metalled roads, representing tremendous capital investment in transport. This brought ample returns by enabling the potential of the horse to be developed in full.

It is sometimes said that the coming of the railway marked the end of the coach era. While this was undoubtedly true for the long-distance routes, which could not compete with the speed of the train and went out of business, the railway age brought new opportunities in the remoter parts of the country such as Exmoor. Many passengers arriving at the railhead still had a considerable distance to travel to their ultimate destination. Coach operators were quick to seize upon this and 'feeder' services, linking towns distant from the railway with the nearest station, enabled the travellers to complete their journey.

Such routes often adapted to changing circumstances. As the railway

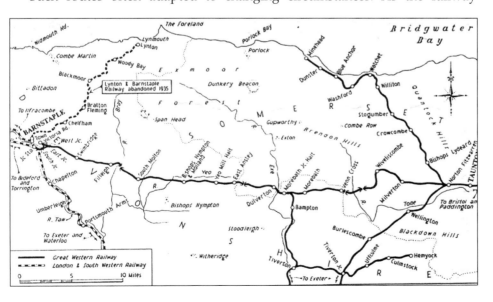

network spread westward, the coach services altered accordingly. Around Exmoor the pace of change was relatively slow. From the arrival of the Bristol and West Railway at Bridgwater in July, 1841 it took 32 years for the rails to reach Minehead. Barnstaple rejoiced in the coming of the railway in 1854 but another 44 years elapsed before Lynton saw a train. In the mean time coaches maintained connections between town and railhead.

Those travelling to the Exmoor area by land could approach from the east, the west of the south.

From the East – Minehead, Lynton and Lynmouth

In the pre-railway days the traveller from Minehead had the choice of two conveyances. Three days each week a coach left the Plume of Feathers for Bridgwater, returning the following day. Opposition was provided by the mail coaches which, from about the late 1820s, ran daily to and from Taunton, allowing connections to all parts of the country. Their starting point was directly opposite at the rival Wellington Inn.

The state of the road had been a barrier to coach travel west of Minehead

Wellington Square, Minehead, dominated by the large tree. On the right is the Plume of Feathers and on the far left the other coaching hotel, from which the square gets its name. The absence of traffic and the sauntering pedestrians are in sharp contrast with modern use of the square. The solitary street light would have produced only token illumination after dark. (PC)

and the links between Lynton and Lynmouth and the outside world had been by sea, or landward to the west, via Barnstaple. But with some improvements to the high moorland road between Porlock and Countisbury and following the opening of the broad-gauge railway between Bristol and Bridgwater in 1841, a new coach service was inaugurated from Lynton and Lynmouth to connect with the trains at Bridgwater station. This enabled passengers to reach Lynton and Lynmouth from the east, although the state of the roads in winter precluded operation between the autumn and the following spring. When the railway was extended through Taunton to Exeter, the coach link with Bridgwater continued, connections being made at Minehead to and from Taunton.

A local guidebook stated:

During the summer months only, from the beginning of June to the middle of October, a coach runs daily from Lynton (starting at 6 o'clock and returning at half past eight), through Porlock, Minehead and Dunster to Bridgwater; another meets this coach at Minehead for Taunton; both arriving at their respective destinations in time to meet the Express Train from Exeter to London. They start again on their homeward journey upon the arrival of the Express Down Train from London. The fare is twelve shillings on the outside and twenty shillings inside.

At Lynton and Lynmouth those with accommodation to let competed for the custom of visitors. The approach from Minehead, being down Countisbury Hill, gave the waiting hotel-keepers early warning of a potential customer. The guide continued:

> At Lynmouth telescopes are employed at the rival houses for the prompt discovery of the approaching traveller. He had better, therefore, determine beforehand on his inn, or he will become a bone of contention to a triad of post boys, who wait with additional horses at the bottom of the hill to drag the carriage to its destination.
>
> Where parties prefer the one or the other (Hotel) they should insist upon being taken or driven to the one they desire, regardless of the strongly expressed wish of the post boys or the porters of the coach to gain the customers for their employer's Hotel; firmness on the part of the Visitor would soon remedy an evil much complained of. Carriages from Minehead are seen some miles before they arrive in Lynmouth, so that Hotels are enabled to send a spare horse to help the carriage up the hill to Lynton, if required, free of charge to the party.
>
> The local time, it should be observed, is nearly twenty minutes slower than the London time kept by the Post Office.

It was perhaps the need to ensure that hotel beds were filled that led the Lynton hoteliers to play a prominent part in the coach trade. For, if one conveyed the passenger to the resort, there was an advantage in ensuring that the visitor stayed in the proprietor's premises.

The route between Porlock and Lynmouth was a considerable challenge due to the state of the roads, the steep hills to be ascended and descended and, sometimes, the condition of the driver! Many of the early coachmen enjoyed a drink and W.H. Thornton, in his *Reminiscences and Reflections of an Old West-Country Clergyman*, gives an amusing account of a coach trip between Lynton and Bridgwater station in the 1850s. He was going to meet two relatives and the coach was driven by a man named Warwell:

> We left Lynton at about six am and Warwell had beer at Countisbury, beer again at Porlock, Minehead, Dunster, Williton, Putsham and Cannington. What he consumed in the couple of hours during which the coach waited at Bridgwater I do not know but on the return journey he had hot spirits at every place where in the forenoon he had called for beer. We reached Lynton at about 10pm and he congratulated himself to me on his self-restraint in the matter of drink. He never took spirits until he turned backwards, as some people did; but he could never abide their drinking ways, he said.

The above tale should be considered in the context of the conditions under which the old coachmen worked. They sat high up on the box, open to the elements as they drove along a road over 1000 feet above sea-level. Exposed to gales from the Bristol Channel, wind, rain and snow sweeping in off the moor, they sat huddled in several layers of clothing trying to avoid freezing to death. Perhaps it was no wonder that they fortified themselves against the cold at every opportunity.

Minehead station, with various horse-drawn conveyances. An enclosed horse bus conveyed guests to and from their hotel, a two-horse brake and a charabanc catered for excursionists to Exmoor and the four-in-hand coach covered the arduous 20-mile trip to Lynmouth and Lynton. (KA)

Minehead. The Square is virtually devoid of traffic as the coach, with a good load of passengers, passes the Plume of Feathers. At the rear, the guard keeps an anxious look-out. Floyd's Stationers and Fancy Draper's shop can be seen to the left of the coach and the Wellington Hotel is just in view. (PC)

In the 1860s, in addition to the coach linking Lynton and Lynmouth with the railway, two conveyances also plied between the Wellington Hotel, Minehead and Williton station. They were the 'Prince of Wales' and the 'Pilot' and it would appear that they continued until the tracks were extended to Minehead.

As the railway builders pushed west and the West Somerset Railway was constructed between Taunton and Minehead, so the coach routes were shortened to link at the railhead. Williton was the terminus from 1862 and twelve years later Minehead was finally reached. 'Corridor and dining trains are run from all the large centres; and even the ordinary third class carriages are most elegant and comfortable,' a local guide declared.

Following the opening of Minehead station in 1874 the road between Minehead and Porlock was served three times daily by four-in-hand coaches and they continued on to Lynmouth and Lynton daily in summer but only one day a week in winter.

The road between Minehead, Lynton and Lynmouth was the most romantic approach to the twin resorts, involving a coach journey of some 18 miles. It was also arduous for both man and beast. From Minehead to Porlock was a comparatively level and lowland course of 6 miles and a stop was made at the Ship Inn, Porlock, where a third pair of horses were attached for the ascent of Porlock Hill – 1000 feet up in about a mile. When the coach was ready to leave a boy would ride a leading horse. Just before the first bend 'the cooperation of passengers' was sought and all the men of the party were expected to walk up, or at any rate

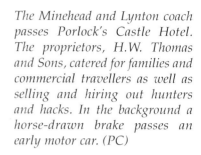

The Minehead and Lynton coach passes Porlock's Castle Hotel. The proprietors, H.W. Thomas and Sons, catered for families and commercial travellers as well as selling and hiring out hunters and hacks. In the background a horse-drawn brake passes an early motor car. (PC)

A busy scene at the Ship Inn, Porlock, as a pair of extra horses are attached ready for the ascent of Porlock Hill. The boy will ride one of the leading horses to the top, where they will be unhitched and taken back to Porlock. Passengers used to throw money to the lad, but if he dismounted to pick up the coins the horses were liable to set off home without him. (RG)

it was deemed merciful to do so. Even so, the hard panting of the tired horses was said to be 'painfully suggestive' for the travellers. If the load was particularly heavy, and much luggage was carried, the call would come for all ladies under 40 years of age to descend and walk. It is said that this usually had the effect of emptying the coach of all female passengers. The coach then continued to just above the second bend and waited for the passengers. When they were all aboard once more, it was onward and upward to the level just above Whitstones. Here the two leaders would be unhitched and the boy thanked and given a tip. The coach went on to Culbone Stables and the boy took the extra horses back to Porlock.

The road surface on the hill provoked much comment. One passenger said that it was reduced to red clay and full of ruts by the frequent use of skid pans. These were placed under the coach wheels to assist braking. In wet weather the surface was slippery, when dry it was rutted and bumpy.

The descent of Porlock Hill must have been a terrifying experience for those of a nervous disposition riding on top. Perched 10 feet or more above the road, with little to prevent a passenger falling over the side, the coach swayed its way down over the precipitous hill, the horses working hard to hold the coach back, the skids being placed under the sliding wheels and several very sharp bends to negotiate. The skids, or drags, were no more than pieces of heavy iron which, when pushed under the wheel, locked it. The coach then virtually slid down the hill and on occasions the skids became so hot that they smoked, much to the alarm of the passengers.

For those travelling to Lynton, the top of Porlock Hill brought them to Culbone Stables, later named Yearner Stables, where the horses were changed. Originally nothing was available here in the way of 'lunch-viands' beyond bread and cheese but later a 'rustic tea' was served on top of the coach.

Then, as a contemporary account tells us:

> away over the high and desolate table land, wild and grand, which extends 'til the horn heralds our approach to Countisbury Hill, on the right the old Church, on the left the Blue Ball Inn. A glimpse to the south of the Lyn below ... and we commence the long and almost alarming descent along the face of the cliff to Lynmouth.

The side of the road was at one time unguarded but later a low stone wall separated it from the precipitous drop to the sea.

Walter Klickmann, who travelled two hundred miles by coach, from Minehead to Land's End, in the early part of the twentieth century, described the start of his journey thus:

As two passengers walk up the hill behind their carriage, two coach-loads descend. The coachmen keep to the right in order to take a sweep round the bend as the high centre of gravity meant overturning was a very real danger. (KA)

The afternoon coach from Minehead to Lynmouth is well known as a smart and serviceable turn-out. It is, and has need to be, well horsed for the country's face in these parts has protuberances akin to young mountains. An easy run of six miles brings us to Porlock, so reminiscent of Whyte-Melville's spirited romance 'Katerfelto'. Here the serious work of the stage begins, and in another mile we are 1400 feet above sea level. As every cyclist knows, though sometimes he doubts, there are two sides to every hill and a long gentle decline leads through County Gate into Devonshire, and so on to Lynmouth. Away on the left lies the famous Doone Valley, and the passengers listen respectfully while the whip and guard declaim abridged versions of *Lorna Doone*. We drop steeply into Lynmouth with musical flourishes on the horn and a verbal contrapuntal treatment composed of 'Oh, isn't that...' (the range of adjectives is too large to quote).

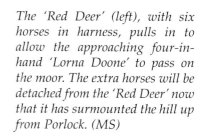

The 'Red Deer' (left), with six horses in harness, pulls in to allow the approaching four-in-hand 'Lorna Doone' to pass on the moor. The extra horses will be detached from the 'Red Deer' now that it has surmounted the hill up from Porlock. (MS)

Countisbury, the Coach at the Blue Ball Inn. The top-hatted driver has just dismounted after climbing Countisbury Hill from Lynmouth and the two greys at the front will now be detached and the man will ride them back to the stables. (PC)

In Lynmouth a halt was called at the Lyndale Hotel, by the bridge spanning the Lyn, for the Lynmouth passengers to alight. Then struggling up the steep hill to Lynton, the terminus was reached.

The journey between Minehead and Lynton took some three hours. On a fine summer's day it must have been a delight and one of the most notable coach journeys in the land. However, in winter when snow lay or it was cold, it must have been an experience to be endured, not enjoyed.

The principal owner of coaches on the Lynton–Minehead route was Thomas Baker, who seems to have pioneered the horse-drawn service over the hills of Countisbury and Porlock. He was a Lynton man who adapted to changing times. His father was a farmer and carrier, using packhorses to convey lime and coal. Starting as a farmer and shipowner, Thomas became a successful hotelier. He played a prominent part in the local community, rearing Exmoor ponies and hunting into old age. His coach, named 'Lorna Doone', left Lynton in the morning and returned from Minehead in the afternoon, connecting with the principal train services to and from London. It was thus the route used mainly by long distance travellers.

Thomas Baker was also the proprietor of the Castle Hotel and Family Boarding House. This had been greatly improved, and was 'replete with every comfort and convenience for families visiting this romantic neighbourhood'. It was patronised by H.R.H. The Prince of Wales and the name was then changed to the 'Royal Castle'. Thomas Baker senior died in 1890 at the age of 86, having been succeeded in later years by his son, upon whose retirement, control of the hotel and coaching business passed to Tom Jones of Lynton, a man with many and varied business interests. Running in competition with the 'Lorna Doone'

Some of the older and younger passengers on the Minehead coach ride up Countisbury Hill, while the others trudge along behind, accompanied by a uniformed man pushing his bicycle. (PC)

Spot the difference! In the tourism business, competition was particularly intense in Lynton and Lynmouth. The Royal Castle Hotel, unrestrained by trades description legislation, adapted the photograph above, a masterpiece of the photographer's art of deception. The only authentic part of the view is the coach on Countisbury Hill. The Royal Castle has been placed in a totally fictitious position, the opposition establishments at Lynton have been obliterated behind a non-existent wood, while the charms of Lynmouth harbour have been grafted on from another picture. (PC)

A Lynton and Minehead coach (a 'smart turn-out' with its elegant paintwork and lettering and top-hatted driver) prepares to leave Bevan's Lyndale Hotel, one of the best-known establishments in Lynmouth, for the climb up Countisbury. (PC)

was the 'Valley of Rocks' coach, this taking its name from the Lynton hotel owned by its proprietor.

Another coach appeared, starting from Minehead after the arrival of the train due at approximately 9am and returning from Lynton at 4.30pm, enabling visitors and others to connect with the 8.50pm train from Minehead. This coach, known as the 'Red Deer', provided a means of making a day excursion to Lynton from Minehead and stations down the line. At first it was owned by Preedy and Clark of Shute Farm, Minehead, but later passed to a partnership of Preedy and Thristle of the Plume of Feathers yard, Minehead. It was acquired by Harold Langdon in the early years of the twentieth century. The fare for the double journey was eleven shillings and sixpence, or for a single trip seven shillings and sixpence.

Well-known drivers of the Lynton–Minehead coaches were William Vellacott, Edward and Tom Baker, John Curtis, George Chugg, John Hussell and Ned Carey. The last named became a driver on the Cliff Railway and died, aged 85, in 1959.

The four-in-hand service was not an easy business to manage. Although considerable numbers were conveyed each year – in the 1890s over 3600 on the 'Lorna Doone' and 1500 on the 'Red Deer' – the number of passengers presenting themselves for travel on any departure could vary tremendously and when numbers were large the necessary coaches and horses had to be found quickly. At Easter 1914, for example, the Minehead coach had to be supplemented by three large horse-drawn charabancs. There were also considerable numbers of animals required to allow for changes at Culbone and additional beasts to help the coach up over both Porlock and Countisbury. Added to this was the seasonal nature of the service and it is no wonder that there were many changes in ownership over the years.

The horse-drawn coaches continued to run until after the Great War of 1914–18, long after many of their contemporaries had given way to motor traction. When motor charabancs first reached Exmoor, Porlock and Countisbury Hills were considered too dangerous for the newfangled motors with their somewhat inadequate braking systems. The sound of 'Anchors Aweigh' still rang out from the post horn of the red-coated guard, Mr Carey, until, in 1920, the ubiquitous motor inevitably replaced the grand old Lynton and Minehead coach. The new motors, which retained for a time the old names of the coaches, 'Lorna Doone' and 'Red Deer' were advertised as 'Cars DeLuxe, driven by a chauffeur who has his business at his finger tips'.

But the old coaches did not instantly fade away. In 1920 one of the Lynton and Minehead four-in-hand stagecoaches was used as the bridal coach of Mr C. Carey (the guard) and his bride after the marriage ceremony, which took place at Lynton. As late as 1925 the *North Devon Journal* reported that at Lynton and Lynmouth:

> Automobile traffic has, in the main, driven the horse off the road – indeed it is believed there are only two or three horse-drawn vehicles regularly on hire in both places. Lovers of the old stagecoach, with driver, guard and horn, and the four clinking steeds will be glad to know that Mr Tom Jones, the owner, intends to resume its excursions to the different points shortly. The interest this feature of the past arouses is great, and the coach is always full of occupants. This is not to be wondered at when it is realised it is the identical one formerly running to Minehead and not a 'slip up' new one belonging to a London or Brighton Coaching Club.

But the resurgence did not last long and within a few years motors reigned supreme. The old four-horsed coach with liveried driver and guard and the music of the horn was no more. Coaching days were gone for ever.

From the West – Barnstaple and Ilfracombe to Lynton

As the road between Lynton and Barnstaple was improved during the early nineteenth century, a conveyance began running regularly between the two places. By 1830 Charles Fry's vehicle left Lynton every Tuesday and Friday for the Wellington Arms, Barnstaple, returning the same afternoon. This provided a means of access to Barnstaple Market and also allowed travellers to continue the next day to other parts of the country. The 'Royal Mail' coach from Ilfracombe left the Royal and Fortescue, Barnstaple, for Reading and London every morning at six. Its competitor, the 'North Devon Telegraph', left the Golden Lion daily at half-past seven but took the road via Salisbury to London. A link with South Devon was by the coach 'North Devon', which left the Golden Lion every Monday, Wednesday and Friday morning at half-past seven and went through Bideford, Torrington, Hatherleigh and Okehampton to Plymouth.

By 1850 the Lynton service was in the hands of William Richards. His omnibus carried the mails, leaving Lynton Post Office on Tuesday and Friday at 6am, reaching Barnstaple in time for the Plymouth and Tiverton coaches. The return journey left the King's Arms, Barnstaple the same afternoon at 3 o'clock and the fare was two shillings and sixpence.

On 12 July 1854 the North Devon Railway from Exeter to Barnstaple opened. In an unfortunate incident only half the special train carrying dignitaries from Exeter arrived on schedule. The remainder had inadvertently been left behind at Umberleigh! Richards' omnibus now provided the link between Lynton and Lynmouth and the railway system. In addition to running the omnibus William Richards was the local sub-agent for the Railway company, beer retailer, seed, manure and insurance agent and lodging-house keeper at Lynton. In Barnstaple the terminus was now situated at the offices of the principal agents of the Railway, Messrs Pridham and Lake, in Joy Street.

Although the road between Lynton and Barnstaple had been improved it was still not good and this led to complaints that it was almost impassable and highly dangerous to passengers. However, this did not stop the services to and from Lynton being increased to cope with the extra numbers travelling as a consequence of the opening of the railway. Soon the Lynton omnibus to Barnstaple ran daily in summer and three times a week in winter, and a further conveyance linked Lynton with Ilfracombe during the summer months.

The various omnibuses and coaches seem to have changed hands at regular intervals. The one operating between Lynton and Barnstaple passed to John Crook, for many years the proprietor of the Valley of Rocks Hotel which offered 'Luxurious suites of Private Apartments, elegant Salle à manger, Ladies' Drawing Room and wines of the choicest vintage'. After extensive additions and improvements it combined 'moderate charges with all necessary means of accommodation and comfort of families and tourists'. John Crook had a hand with Thomas Baker in starting the coach link to and from the West Somerset Railway and was held in high esteem locally. He learned to drive a motor after he became a nonagenarian and died at the age of 96 in 1923. Another venture in which he at one time had an interest was the Crown Commercial and Family Hotel and Posting House, Lynton.

The successors to John Crook on the Lynton and Barnstaple route were Jones Brothers of Lynton. They introduced the well-appointed, fast four-horse coach 'Tantivvy'. During the summer this was supplemented by the 'Glen Lynn' and the 'Tally Ho!' In the season there were three return journeys to Barnstaple daily, leaving Lynton at 8am, 11am and 3pm, each coach carrying up to 20 passengers and their luggage. The horses were changed at Loxhore in both directions and an extra animal would be attached to help drag the coach up Loxhore Hill.

LYNTON, LYNMOUTH, AND BARNSTAPLE.

THE WELL-APPOINTED FAST FOUR-HORSE COACH,

"TANTIVY,"

carrying the mails, runs daily throughout the year (Sundays excepted), in connection with the trains of London and South-Western Railway.

THE ONLY DAILY ROUTE THROUGHOUT THE YEAR FROM AND TO LYNTON AND LYNMOUTH.

The "GLEN LYN" and the "TALLY HO!"

Additional Coaches run during the SUMMER SEASON ONLY.

		A.M.	P.M.	P.M.		TO LYNTON.		
MESSRS. JONES BROS.' FAST FOUR-HORSE COACHES ...	"TANTIVY," (all the year round) dep.	8 0	...	...	The Coaches meet Trains at Barnstaple Junction.			
	"GLEN LYN," during the sum-	...	1 45	...		A.M.	A.M.	A.M.
	"TALLY HO!" mer season only	...	...	5 0				
FROM LYNTON	Barnstaple Junc. arr.	11 0	3 0	8 0	WATERLOO LONDON dep.	...	9 5	11 0
	TRAINS—				Portsmouth ...... "	...	8 0	10 40
Via LONDON AND SOUTH WESTERN RAILWAY.	Barnstaple Junction ......dep.	11 13	3 21	8 17	Southampton ...... "	...	8 25	11 33
	Okehampton.........arr.	2 44	5 12	10 22	Salisbury .... "	...	11 23	1 5
COACHES leave the Company's Booking Offices, Churchill, Lynton, every Week-day.	Launceston (*via* Halwill)	4 0	9 32	...	Exeter (Queen St.)... "	6 50	1 45	3 20
	Tavistock .... "	3 15	5 49	10 48	Plymouth (North Rd.) "	...	11 42	...
	Plymouth (North Rd.) "	3 42	6 30	11 16	Tavistock .... "	...	12 31	...
THROUGH BOOKING.— Passengers can book to Lynton from stations on this system.	Exeter (Queen St.)......... "	12 39	4 54	9 57	Launceston(*via* Halwill)	...	10 15	...
	Salisbury .... "	2 49	8 3	...	Okehampton .... "	...	1 9	...
	Southampton .... "	5 26	10 12	...	Barnstaple Junction arr.	8 23	3 21	4 33
	Portsmouth .... "	6 30	10 56	...	COACH.— Barnstaple			
	WATERLOO LONDON arrive	5 0	10 15	...	LYNTON Junc. dep	8 25	3 35	5 0
					Lynton arr.	11 0	6 30	7 40

In winter a smaller three-horse vehicle was used to maintain the service. As the mails were carried it was imperative that the coach got through, irrespective of how bad the conditions were in the hilly, difficult country encountered between the two places. The fare between Lynton and Barnstaple was six shillings single, seven shillings and sixpence return, with an extra shilling for those travelling inside or on the box. In a full year during the 1890s some 7000 people were carried and it was the main route to and from the resorts for long-distance travellers. The drivers, who were all great characters, included George Moon, Tom Willis and John Baker. The latter became stationmaster at Chelfham after the opening of the light railway. Others who worked at the Coach office were W. Bowden, R. Thorne, T. Reeves, W. Way and T. Esson.

The firm of Jones Brothers were well known in Lynton and played a prominent part in the development of both townships. They could supply you with a house and its total equipment in ironmongery, furniture and every essential, and if you wanted to attend business at Barnstaple, Minehead or South Molton their coaches or other vehicles (always splendidly horsed) conveyed you thither. If you decided to buy a cottage, house or mansion, or if a lighthouse, church or public hall had to be erected, Jones Brothers could and did carry out the work eminently satisfactorily. The three brothers, 'Mr Tom', 'Mr Bob' and 'Mr Jack', were entrepreneurs who made a considerable contribution to the development of Lynton. Tom was a Justice of the Peace, Chairman of Lynton

Urban District Council and a member of the Barnstaple Board of Guardians. Bob Jones designed the Cliff Railway, the first of its kind, and also built the Foreland Lighthouse. It was Jones Brothers who supplied between sixteen and twenty horses, in the charge of Tom Willis, to pull the Lynmouth lifeboat 13 miles overland to Porlock, the only place it could be launched, in severe storms in January 1899. The epic rescue of the full-rigged sailing vessel *Forest Hall* won lasting fame for the Lynmouth lifeboat crew and their helpers.

Jones Brothers were pre-eminent in coaching at the resort, their office by the church being the place to book a trip. In the words of a local guidebook:

> There is only one coaching establishment at Lynton and this is Mr Tom Jones'. His office cannot be missed and the excursions he runs are items which go to make up the enjoyment of the holiday. The list of excursion trips is too extensive to be put into a short paragraph but a list is easily obtainable at the office.

In the early days Lynton Hill was considered too dangerous for motors, so drivers used the Cliff Railway. Built in 1890 to link Lynton and Lynmouth, it was the first of its kind in the country.(PC)

One of their coachmen achieved a degree of fame in later years. John Latham was born at Lynn Bridge, near Lynton, and worked for Tom Jones for many years. Probably as a result of a conversation with a visitor he obtained employment in a London livery stable. Here he came into contact with Mr Charles W. Meyer of Philadelphia, who wanted 'someone to blow the horn on his coach'. John Latham soon convinced Mr Meyer of his capabilities in this respect and went to the United States with him.

Meyer, known as Judge Meyer, was a lawyer and his stable was, according to Latham, one of the best. After giving up law he went in for stockbroking but his financial operations went astray and the time came when he could no longer keep up his horses. In about 1908 John Latham was dismissed and at the time back wages were owing to him. He somehow made his way back to England, leaving the debt on record before his departure.

In England his circumstances were not fortunate and with his wife and son he tramped the country. His wife ultimately went into service and he lost touch with her. By the early 1930s, when he was 65 years old, he and his young son, then aged ten, had been in the Barnstaple Workhouse for about six years when news came that Mr Meyer had come into an inheritance of £100,000 and that John Latham's claim for back wages was to be met. A money draft was received soon afterwards, and the amount was not the £600 claimed, but £1025, owing to the payment being made in American dollars and the current favourable exchange rate. When asked by the local press what he intended to do, John Latham replied that he hardly knew. He had, however, been very comfortable in the institution and was grateful to the Master, Mr E. George, and his staff. He later added that he would like 'to fly to America'.

On hearing of John Latham's good fortune and possible intentions Barnstaple Guardian's Committee were greatly exercised. Asking what work he did, they received the reply: 'Very little'. During their considerations they retained the money draft and in their minds was the fact that Latham and his son had cost them 30 shillings (£1.50) a week for six years, a total of £468. Some members thought he would soon spend the lot; others considered that he was entitled to use the money as he wished. Mr C.F. Dart asked, amid laughter, if there had been any inducement to get Latham to remain at the institution and get him to invest his money in Workhouse Bonds.

Eventually it was agreed to pay John Latham £600, being the amount of his original claim, and to retain £425 as a contribution to the cost of caring for him and his son. The clerk was asked to make any inducement possible to get John Latham to use the money in the best possible way but what became of him has not yet been discovered.

For twenty years schemes designed to secure railway communication with Lynton were put before the public. Several Acts of Parliament were obtained but nothing came of any of them until a scheme launched by Sir George Newnes, Baronet, and several gentlemen interested in Lynton received parliamentary sanction. Work commenced and in 1898 the Lynton and Barnstaple coaches were superseded by a light railway. The narrow gauge meant a change of trains was necessary at Barnstaple Town Station and then it took over an hour and a three-quarters to cover the 19 miles to Lynton. One contemporary reporter commented that a hearse could have done it in less time. On reaching Lynton terminus, passengers were a good mile away from the town and the principal hotels by a very steep road and had to resort to a horse-drawn omnibus (fare one shilling), run by Tom Jones, for the final stage of the journey.

A contemporary report noted:

Sixty years ago (in the 1830s) the Barumite who wished to visit London had to be prepared to devote nearly £5 to travelling, and to spend practically sixty hours in a coach. Travelling was then the privilege of the few. Today the busy trader can perform the trip with less than twelve hours' travelling and at an expenditure of £1.15s. – reduced to half this amount

The beginning of the end for horse-drawn transport. A crowd turns out to see the last coach on the Barnstaple and Lynton route, 10 May 1898. (EPA)

during the excursion season.... The Victorian Era has produced no more wonderful, no more wholesome development.

Although the railway undoubtedly brought great improvements, long-distance passengers to or from Lynton still faced a lengthy journey with a change at Barnstaple. As motor traffic increased after the Great War the little Lynton and Barnstaple trains, although delightfully picturesque and so in accord with the hill country they served, found it hard to compete with travel by road and the line finally closed in 1935 after a relatively short life of only 37 years.

The other route westward for passengers in and out of Lynton was via Ilfracombe. By 1850 William Crook of Lynton was running a regular conveyance during the months of June, July, August and September. This left the Crown Hotel, Lynton, on Mondays, Wednesdays and Fridays at 11am, returning the following day from the Clarence Hotel, Ilfracombe. Fares were four shillings outside, five shillings inside.

One traveller describing his journey from Lynmouth to Ilfracombe said:

Eight am in summer as a starting time is an hour quite conformable with healthy inclinations. Having ascended by the 'Tit Bits' railway from Lynmouth ... we say 'Good-bye' to one of the fairest spots in England. The Ilfracombe coach, as it leaves Lynton, follows the West Lyn. At Martinhoe Cross the driver turns himself into an animated foot-rule and mentions that we have topped 1000 feet. Parracombe and Kentisbury Downs likewise need plenty of collar work.... Combmartin Bay is always admirable, and we closely follow the cliffs to Ilfracombe, so beloved of honeymooners.

However, the majority of traffic on this route originated at the Ilfracombe end and consisted of visitors staying in the town and visting Lynton and Lynmouth for the day. As coaching developed two names above all others came to be connected with the Lynton excursion coaches from Ilfracombe. 'Who does not know Sam Colwill, the veteran North Devon whip, who for more than twenty years drove the coach that ran between Ilfracombe and Old Barum (Barnstaple) in the anti railway times....' So started an article in the *Ilfracombe Chronicle* of 1896, continuing:

Ilfracombe was popular with Victorian visitors and a holiday invariably included a day excursion to Lynton and Lynmouth. The two main coach proprietors, Thomas Copp and Sam Colwill, vied to present the finest spectacle. Here Sam Colwill stands proudly in front of his coach, 'The Magnet', while his son is at the reins. (CPC)

Well, time brings changes to all of us and so it has to Sam Colwill. Like the Sultan of Turkey a revolution has quietly removed him from his throne – the box seat – and deposited him where he did not expect to find himself.

The opening of the railway had, in fact, deprived him of his employment but he began to keep his own carriage and began running a regular excursion brake from Ilfracombe to Lynton and Lynmouth each day. He gradually expanded his business into the supply of post horses, carriages, wagonettes, etc.

Colwill is an old servant of the public and has served them unfailingly in fair weather and foul ... and only asks for the chance to get a living for his wife and family. It is hoped that residents will extend to Sam a helping hand and a kindly word of encouragement, while we will ask lodging house keepers to recommend Colwill's Lynton daily Excursion Brake.

Sam Colwill had shrewdly observed the potential appeal of a trip to the romantic scenery of Lynton and Lynmouth. He was a first-class horseman, to whom testimonials appeared in many publications. His smart four-in-hand coach, the 'Benita' (named after Benita Odam, Lorna Doone's nurse), became well known and, for many, an essential part of a stay in Ilfracombe was an excursion on the 'Benita'. Every morning, 'with the guard blowing his horn to clear the road of the many carts that obstruct our narrow thoroughfares', the coach with its team of greys would sweep out of town, always drawing an admiring crowd to see it on its way. Horses were changed at the half-way point, passengers remaining on board while this happened.

It is not surprising that he was able to introduce a second coach, 'The Magnet', for his son Tom to drive. 'From the Ilfracombe office of this reliable firm' enjoyable trips were run daily to all places of interest in the district, such as Watermouth Caves, Berrynarbor and the Sterrage Valley and to Lee Beach. Wagonettes and three- or four-horse charabancs were available for picnic parties and post horses were available on hire.

Sam Colwill published a small booklet entitled 'English Switzerland, How to spend a day at Lynton and Lynmouth' and a copy was given to every passenger. Such was his fame and popularity that a song 'Coachman Sam, On the Lynton Road in the Morning' was written, with words by Will H. Coates and music by Allen T. Hussell. This was published as sheet music and the first verse began:

I'll sing you a song of the olden days,
The coaching days, the golden days,
Of Coachman Sam and his team of greys,
On the Lynton road in the morning.

Tom Colwill took over from his father and, like him, he was full of stories with which he regaled his passengers. Tom took great care of his horses, calling them his 'dears and darlings' and, according to a visiting reporter, he talked to them 'like rational beings'. Regrettably he was killed in a coaching accident and his sister, Laura, then managed the business. When their main competitors in Ilfracombe started to use motors in 1910 Colwill's refused to follow suit and their horse-drawn coaches continued until the Great War. In 1920 the firm finally embraced motor traction with Colwill's Motor Services, 'The Grey Fleet of Arm-chair Chars-a-banc de Luxe' running daily motor tours and motor omnibus services were inaugurated over a wide area of North Devon. The business was sold to James Hardy of Minehead in 1924 and he, mindful of the goodwill attached to the family name, thereafter used the title Hardy-Colwill's for his operations.

The great rival of the Colwills was Thomas Copp. His coaches – 'Alert', 'Defiance' and 'Katerfelto' – were, like Colwill's, superbly turned out. His starting point was opposite that of Colwill's and both vied to present the finest spectacle. Liveried coachmen and guards, good horses and decorative coaches were all designed to attract the attention of the traveller and lure them to the owner's service and away from the opposition.

Thomas Copp's splendidly liveried coachman at the reins of a coach about to leave the Royal Clarence Hotel, Ilfracombe, for Lynton, known as 'The English Switzerland'. (RG)

At various times Tom Copp had been in partnership with three different people, all of whom had been connected with the Royal Clarence Hotel, Ilfracombe: Messrs Clemow, Lake and Carthew. He then set up on his own account and his coaches were said to be the only ones that conveyed the Great Western and London and South Western Railway Tourist Ticket passengers. He built up a considerable posting establishment, including a station bus, hearse and mourning carriages. Although he was not perhaps quite the figure of folklore as his rival, Thomas Copp carried two-thirds of the passengers on the Lynton Excursion Coaches. In 1910 he partially adopted motor traffic and disposed of some of his horses and carriages. The local press noted:

It is, of course, manifest that from the hilly nature of the locality some places must probably still be served by the old and delightful style of (horse-drawn) coaches or chars-a-banc, so that we shall still, in all probability, hear the musical sound of the coach horn in season.

Indeed the horse-drawn vehicles also catered for those passengers nervous of the newfangled method of transport. On an early motor outing 35 girl swimmers who had earned Swimming Club medals were conveyed by 'one of Mr Thomas Copp's fine motors' (which were known as the 'Silver Cars'). Mr Bruce

Copp, his son, was in charge 'and by his very careful driving showed he felt the responsibility of having so many lady passengers'.

The motor vehicles were commandeered during the First World War but services recommenced after hostilities and, in 1920, Tom Copp decided that the future lay entirely with motors. He sold off his six landaus, three Victorias, two pair-horse brakes, three single-horse wagonettes, six pair-horse charabancs, one nearly new coach, one station omnibus, a dog cart, a hay cart, a dung cart, harness for 26 horses and sundry equipment. In 1924, with competition from larger companies increasing, the business of Thomas Copp and Son merged with the old-established firm of Autocars to become Copps and Autocars (Ilfracombe) Ltd.

The Ilfracombe coaches to Lynton carried considerable numbers of people, some 16,000 a year during the 1890s. This represented nearly 40 per cent of all visitors to Lynton and compared with 7000 on the Barnstaple service and 5000 on the Minehead route. The majority of the long-stay visitors came by rail and then on the Barnstaple or Minehead coaches, whereas the traffic to and from Ilfracombe was mainly day excursionists.

The proud driver of W.H. Gubb's horse-drawn conveyance, wearing a long coat and top hat and holding the whip, prepares to take an elegant private party on an excursion from Ilfracombe. (RG)

An afternoon outing from Ilfracombe to the Sterrage Valley via the new Barnstaple road through the woods, returning via Berrynarbor and Watermouth Castle, cost half a crown in 1916. (PC)

At the height of the coaching days in 1890 there was a coach from Lynton to Ilfracombe every morning (Lake and Copp's 'Dreadnought'), then in late afternoon five different services which had come out from Ilfracombe in the morning returned to the resort. The 'Defiance' and 'Katerfelto' belonged to Lake and Copp, the 'Teazer' was owned by Loverings and there was Sam Colwill's 'Benita'.

Although motor transport had played a part in excursions from Ilfracombe from 1910 onwards, motor operation ceased during the latter part of the First World War. It was not until 1919 that motor charabancs appeared in numbers and it became obvious that the days of horse traction were numbered. Within two years virtually all the Ilfracombe to Lynton excursion coaches were motor-powered and the 'rollicking galloping coach days', when 'the horn's merry note rang out cheerily' had been replaced by noisy, smelly motors with a somewhat less musical bulb horn.

There had been a previous, though short-lived, attempt to partially replace horse-drawn conveyances with motors. Following the opening of the Lynton and Barnstaple Railway, the directors wished to attract some of the Ilfracombe summer traffic. They saw that an immense number of people went to Lynton for the day from Ilfracombe and that a large proportion of them made the journey all the way by road, few apparently seeing any advantage in changing to the railway at Blackmoor Gate, from where road and rail ran parallel to Lynton. The chairman of the railway, Sir George Newnes, agreed to provide a

Parracombe. Near Ilfracombe.

motor coach connecting link between Ilfracombe and Blackmoor Gate station which it was hoped would entice passengers to travel by motor and train rather than by the rival horse-drawn excursion vehicles. The railway directors felt that by this means passengers would be able to go from Ilfracombe to Lynton and back for considerably less money than the former rates and in half the time. They hoped and believed that the service would bring a substantial increase to the revenue of the company.

Two Milnes-Daimlers were put into service in May 1903, taking the route via Berrydown to avoid the long climb out of Combe Martin. However, the vehicles had to tackle a steep ascent out of Ilfracombe and, in order to keep to the scheduled journey time and maintain connections with the trains, time lost ascending the hill was made up on the level stretch of route. The then maximum permitted speed of 8 miles an hour was frequently exceeded and, following warnings, the police successfully set up a speed trap. The chauffeurs were prosecuted and in July heavily fined (£3) for driving 'a little over' the limit. Sir George thought he was being discriminated against and immediately telegraphed instructions that the service was to be withdrawn. He sold the motors to the Great Western Railway for use in Cornwall.

From the South – Dulverton to Lynton and Minehead

After the Great Western Railway line between Tiverton and Dulverton opened in 1884, the GWR came to an agreement whereby a coach began running on Mondays, Wednesdays and Fridays during the summer months between Dulverton station and Lynton. This considerably shortened the journey from stations in the Exe Valley to and from Lynton and Lynmouth and avoided the necessity to go by way of Barnstaple or Exeter. It also precluded a few passengers from travelling on the rival London and South Western trains through Exeter and Barnstaple.

A partnership of Messrs Charles W. Nelder of the Carnarvon Arms, Brushford, and Thomas Baker of the Castle Hotel, Lynton, provided the 'Tally Ho!' coach. This tackled a route over bad roads and high moorland, with only the small settlement of Simonsbath en route. The numbers travelling were always limited, some 800 to 900 a year, and by 1890 the railway were paying a subsidy of ten shillings a trip for the 20-week season (June to October). However, this was more satisfactory than a coach service between South Molton station and Lynton, which only ran for a few months during 1880 before the GWR decided it could never pay its way and withdrew it.

Dulverton railway station and the Carnarvon Arms Hotel, from the stables of which coach services arrived and departed over the years. The garage in the distance was at one time run by Spencer and Anderson, while the house in the foreground is the family home of the Hawkins. Fred Hawkins operated livery stables and hired out carriages from here until early in the First World War. (EPA)

Between Dulverton and Lynton a stop was made at the Simonsbath Inn, which was run by James Fry and his wife in conjunction with their grocery business. This establishment underwent several changes, the sale of beer and spirits being stopped in 1873 by Frederick Knight, the local landowner and would-be developer of Exmoor. It then became a refreshment house, licensed only to sell wine, but the Frys built up the business and in 1895 it became the William Rufus Hotel. In 1903 the name was changed again, to the Exmoor Forest Hotel, a title familiar to many visitors to the moor.

When Thomas Baker junior retired in 1902 his interest in the 'Tally Ho!' passed to Mr Thomas Sidney Bevan, owner of the Lyndale Hotel and Livery Stables, Lynmouth. This establishment, situated by the Lyndale Bridge under which the East Lyn flowed, was known to visitors the world over and was run by the Bevan family for over 80 years. It was damaged in the Lynmouth flood disaster of 1952 and subsequently demolished, the site now being the Lyndale Car Park. David Arnold, William Vellacott and William Delbridge are recalled as drivers of the 'Tally Ho!', on which a fare of six shillings either way was charged.

The service ceased during the 1914–18 war but was reintroduced for one season in the post-war years, using Tom Jones' motor charabanc 'The Exmoor'. Leaving Lynton at 11am, it arrived at Dulverton station at 1pm for the 1.55pm up train. The return journey left Dulverton at 4.20pm, arriving at Lynton at 6.30pm. Fares had risen to nine shillings single, sixteen shillings return, with passengers to and from Lynmouth conveyed on the Cliff Railway.

A guide published just after the Great War recorded:

The old four horse coach, the 'Tally Ho!', which for a few seasons linked up the 'Lyndale' Hotel, Lynmouth with the 'Carnarvon Arms', Dulverton had to be given up owing to grave defects in the roads, which were too steep or too narrow for fast traffic.... (Now the roads have been improved) a motor coach, run in conjunction with the Great Western Railway, is a regular convenience on the moor during the season – the 'Tally Ho!' over again – but with a difference.

However, the motor service was not a success and it was withdrawn at the end of the first season. In 1924 an attempt by Hardy Central Garage to run a through motor bus service between Ilfracombe, Lynton, Simonsbath, Dulverton and Minehead also failed to last beyond a single summer season.

Another link from the railhead at Dulverton, where connections were made with trains on the Exe Valley line and between Taunton and Barnstaple, was to Dunster and Minehead. In the pre-railway days James Harwood's carriers' van had run between Exeter, Tiverton, Dulverton and Minehead twice a week. The opening of the Exe Valley railway took the passenger traffic on the lower section, but to link Dulverton with the Somerset coast and the West Somerset Railway a four-horse coach, the 'Wild West', ran on Tuesdays, Fridays and Saturdays during the season, leaving the Beach Hotel, adjacent to Minehead station, after the arrival of the train due at 9am. The return was from the Carnarvon Arms, Dulverton station, on the same days at 3pm, connecting with the train leaving Minehead at 7.20pm and in time for dinner at the Minehead hotels and lodging houses. The journey of about 20 miles took some four hours and 'afforded a lovely drive at a moderate cost', five shillings and sixpence single or ten shillings return – box seats one shilling extra.

As well as carrying day excursionists from Minehead, the 'Wild West' catered for railway passengers from Taunton and stations east, who could make a round trip, by train to Minehead, coach to Dulverton and return to their starting point by train, or vice versa. There were also visitors staying in the Dulverton area, attracted by the angling, hunting and natural beauty. One of the best-known hotels was the Carnarvon Arms at Brushford, next to Dulverton station. A contemporary guide stated that its accommodation 'Large though this is and ample enough its stables are, is often taxed to the utmost during the hunting season, when sportsmen from every part of the kingdom assemble'. With alternative accommodation available in the quiet country town of Dulverton, over a mile away, horse-drawn omnibuses from the Lion and the Lamb hotels met every train and provided competitive services for travellers.

The road between Dunster and Dulverton was a hard run for a horse-drawn coach, albeit 'through some of the finest inland scenery in the West Country'. There is a long hill, rough and winding, on the outward run and here was a water trough. On reaching this the horses would drink before the final stage of the climb and, if the road was muddy or icy, the passengers would be invited to descend and walk to the top. At Wheddon Cross, nearly 1000 feet above sea-level, the welcome roadside inn, aptly named 'Rest and Be Thankful', was

The Beach Hotel, Minehead, by the station and the sea front, was the starting point for the 'Wild West' coach to Dulverton. The Lynton coaches also called at the hotel and here a full coachload of passengers pose for the camera before setting off. (MS)

reached. The long run down on the other side kept the horses busy as they held back the weight of the coach, passengers and luggage, then along the bank of the Quarme Water and through the Exe Valley road, with its charming scenery, to reach the terminus at Dulverton station, situated at Brushford.

The 'Wild West' coach appears to have ceased about the time of the Great War and in the post-war years was superseded by a regular service of motor buses.

It is at Brushford that we first come across a family destined to play a leading role in the coaching business around Exmoor: the Hawkins. Fred Hawkins was born in Exeter, married into a well-known family of builders in the city and became a coachman. He is said to have regularly driven along the Exeter–Minehead road and would have been well placed to witness the development of Brushford as a centre for the sporting interests following the arrival of the railway and the building of the Carnarvon Arms Hotel. The opportunities clearly persuaded Fred to set up in business there as a jobmaster and in about 1912 he built a large brick house with outbuildings near the bridge opposite the hotel and station. During the First World War he moved into Minehead. We shall hear more of the family later.

Local Excursions

Visitors staying in the Exmoor area wished to see the beauties of the countryside and the many local places of interest. To allow them to go further afield than was possible on foot, local people provided transport: post horses and carriages of every description. There was also first-class stabling. Early tourists often hired a horse and carriage, in the charge of a knowledgeable local driver, for the exclusive use of their party.

[From Minehead] the hotels arrange for the circular drive to Dunster and Cleeve, returning by Blue Anchor, at nominal fares for each passenger. A carriage to Cloutsham (an exquisite woodland coombe) and back costs about fourteen shillings, or twenty shillings with a pair of horses. This may be combined with the ascent of Dunkery Beacon. A full day's outing (carriage and pair, thirty-five shillings) is to drive via Cutcombe almost to the top of Dunkery, reached by an easy climb of about 250 feet, and back by Luccombe, making the detour to Cloutsham en route. This drive requires a pair of horses.

The 'Pride of the Vale' wagonette, driven by F. Hobbs, outside the Ship Inn, Porlock, while on an excursion from Minehead. (RH)

This extract from a local guide published in the nineteenth century refers to what was to be one of the most popular excursions in the district for many years to come: Dunkery Beacon and Luccombe. This trip remained a firm favourite, not only in the days of horse and carriage but through into the motor age.

As the number of visitors increased, public excursions were also run from Minehead to those places within the range of a day's work for a horse or pair of horses. These allowed those of more modest means to travel, as sharing the conveyance with up to 20 others enabled relatively cheap fares to be charged.

One advertisement of the time reads: 'Drives to Selworthy, Porlock and Porlock Weir. Cheap fares. Hobbs and Co's Brake leaves Minehead station daily at 12 noon for the above places, and returns in time for the 7.15pm up train.' But families or groups of friends were still catered for and 'pleasure parties requiring conveyances' were invited to apply to the company. Staddon's wagonettes and brakes provided a similar service for those desiring to sample the delights of the coast, countryside and moorland and both firms eventually turned to motor traction.

At Lynton and Lynmouth there were similar developments. William Crook, the proprietor of the Crown Hotel and operator of a coach service to and from Ilfracombe, established a posting and horse-letting business. The latter was sold in the 1870s to Charles Medway.

By the 1880s the Pedder family, long associated with Lynton and Lynmouth, had interests in a number of small vessels engaged in the coal trade between South Wales and North Devon, as well as being coal, culm and lime merchants, grocers and drapers, boarding-house and horse and carriage proprietors. They opened a new road linking Lee Road and Lydiate Lane, which became Cross Street, along which building plots were sold. E.J. Pedder had taken over the Crown Hotel from William Crook by 1885 and also its associated posting business, to which he added that of Charles Medway, whose daughter he had married. Edward Pedder is credited with pioneering excursions by brake and wagonette to Malmsmead and the Doone Valley.

The jobmaster's business was sold to Tom Jones of Lynton and the Pedders then took over the Post Office at London House, Lynmouth, from William Crook. At some stage the property was divided, part remaining as the Post Office and the other part becoming the Coaching Office. Edward Pedder received the fateful telegram which called out the Lynmouth lifeboat to the aid of the *Forest Hall* in January 1899. There followed the epic hauling of the lifeboat overland to Porlock, the only place from which it could be launched. Edward Pedder sailed in the rescue boat.

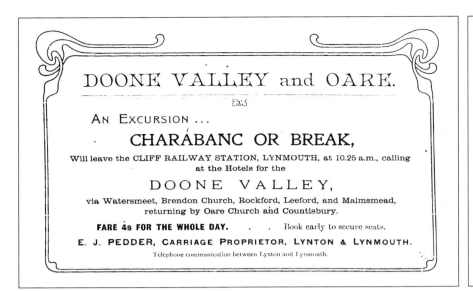
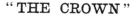

An excursion party sets out up the Watersmeet Road from Lynmouth, with Ned Carey at the reins, on a summer's day. (RG)

At the time of the Lynmouth Flood in 1952 Mr E.J. Pedder, the postmaster, became trapped in a small office which opened off the shop. His schoolboy son, John, showing great presence of mind, smashed the skylight and hoisted his father clear, undoubtedly saving his life.

After purchasing Pedder's brake and wagonette business, Tom Jones further developed the coaching trips from the resorts, running horse-drawn charabancs daily at 11am to the Doone Valley, Hunters Inn via Heddons Mouth and to Simonsbath.

On the Doone Valley trip, the advertisements stated, 'from Hillsford Bridge ... a steep rise [is] climbed and descending by Brendon Church the most beautiful riverine and hill scenery is met with, passing successively Rockford, Millslade, Brendon and Malmsmead, where refreshments may be had for man and beast'. The charabanc 'Exmoor' was used for the trip to 'the excellently appointed' Hunters Inn – a drive unequalled in Devon for bold seascapes and wooded landscapes'. Charabancs also ran to the meets of the Devon and Somerset Stag Hounds at Cloutsham, Yeanor Moor, Brendon Two Gates, and Hawkcombe Head.

For a view of life and travel around Exmoor during the era of the horse, we turn to John Eustace Anderson, who spent a holiday at Minehead during August and September, 1899. He kept a diary and this was published privately, 350 copies being printed. Among his entries we read:

I called at Mr Stoate's premises in Bampton Street at the top of The Avenue where he carries on the business of a jobmaster, and arranged for a drive to Porlock – six miles from here, and then on to Porlock Weir, about a mile further on.

We started at three in the afternoon from The Parade and had a very pretty drive, the country being hilly and well wooded, through Sir Thomas Acland Bart.'s estate. In chatting with the driver I understood that his master, Mr Stoate, farmed about a hundred acres of land and kept a number of horses and a forge. The charge for shoeing in these parts, I understood him to say, was about two shillings.

I thought the Porlock shore was very stony, no sands.... We had tea at The Old Ship Inn, a very countrified house which has an extraordinarily tall white chimney. Some of the cottages were very rustic looking, having pretty flower gardens. The inhabitants appear to be supported by a large tannery in the place and by farm labour.

On the 29th August (in Minehead) I saw several persons in hunting costume, and saw two four-horse coaches start from the station for Lynmouth and Porlock. At noon I observed there were seven bathing machines on wheels at the east side of the bay, black with pitched roofs; also seven curious little slips without wheels, with pitched red roofs. I counted eighteen ladies and girls, and about six men bathing at that time. There appears just now to be one German band in the town which played at different points.

He also noticed an old shepherd on horse back driving half a dozen sheep by the seashore, assisted by his dog. Another dog ran forward barking, but the shepherd's dog did not deign to take any notice. Also noted was a fine young donkey going down to the beach for hire. At the Beach Hotel dogs were allowed in at meals and he saw two ladies who had their dogs sitting demurely on chairs by their sides at the table waiting, he supposed, for 'tit-bits'. 'I saw one very shaggy dog in the room today. I was amused by a gentleman saying to a lady, "Oh what breed is it?" 'Well," says the other, "I suppose it is a Polar bear."'
On Wednesday morning, 30 August 1899, Anderson continues:

We went by a four-horse coach for a twenty mile drive to Lynton from the railway station, having previously booked our seats, at half past nine. Our coachman, John Curtis, was a very broad shouldered, white felt hatted, white water-proofed, taciturn man.

I heard afterwards that he was the landlord of a public house, the 'Stag Hunters', at Brendon, but known by the Lynton people as 'Rockford', as it is built on a rock. He seemed to be given up to his own meditations, both going and coming back. There was a young man assisting him, not in uniform, who acted as guard and blew a horn now and again to test the strength of his lungs, I presume. All Curtis, the coachman, seemed to say on the road was addressed to his horses: 'Get on', 'Come on', Steady now'. There were about twelve of us on the coach, although it would take about twenty, all told.

We were a very quiet party, and rather followed Curtis's example in saying very little to each other. Soon after starting we had two short, sharp showers with a chilly wind over the open Downs.

The hat of a lady, who was sitting alongside the coachman, blew off twice, striking me full in the face, but I caught it each time, otherwise I do not know what would have taken place if old Curtis had had to pull up and wait whilst a chivy was taking place over the Downs after a lady's hat.

When we got to Porlock .... we stopped and all got down to walk up the old Porlock Road to the top. Two horses were put on – one being ridden by a boy as postillion. About a mile up at the top we all got on again, and the two horses were taken off and went back with the boy.

At Culbone stables (nine miles) we stopped and changed the four horses. Whilst there I was amused by Curtis coming out from the stables with a pair of stag horns, which he said belonged to the stableman, who would be willing to sell them. They were handed up to a young man on the roof to look at. 'How much?' says he. 'Thirty shillings' says the stableman, who had just come out. 'No buyer,' promptly answers the gentleman, handing them down again.

In arriving at Lynmouth the scene was pretty, but the beach seems very stony. It lies in a gorge at the bottom of very steep hills.... The coachman used the skid freely going down a very steep road on the edge of the hill, protected by earth banks and a stone wall.... On the side of the cliff (ahead) I noticed a hydraulic lift – which must be of great use.

When we got to the bottom at Lynmouth we all got out at the 'Lyndale' Hotel, and walked up a tremendously steep hill with a sharp turn in it. The Porlock road is not in it for sharpness. A fifth horse was put on to the empty coach, if it could be said to be empty with Curtis on the seat, who now and then considerately invited his horses to 'get on'. At the top we got on and drove to the 'Castle' Hotel, a very large one kept by a Mr Baker, whose father had kept it before him, I was told. He owns the coaches that run between that place and Minehead. We arrived a little after one p.m. in time for lunch having been three and a half hours on the road.

Having ordered a carriage, we drove to Valley of Rocks, so-called, I presume, from some rocks which stand out of the ground. Then we drove to Lyn Glen and walked among some trees in a gorge, and saw the water pouring down over the stones, for which watery sight we paid 4d. each. We were then driven to where the waters meet, and very pretty it is with trees and rustic bridges, etc. We had tea at the 'Lyndale' Hotel at a charge of 9d. each.

At twenty minutes to five p.m. the coach came from Lynton which is, I should say, about four hundred and fifty yards above Lynmouth, and picked us up at the Lyndale Hotel. A fifth horse was put on to drag us up out of Lynmouth.

On the road back we met a gentleman dismounted, his servant holding his horse. He seemed to know Curtis and got on to our coach. On the road back a large hawk or buzzard flew across the road in front of us. The coach does not go the new road because of the trees so overhanging that road. As you come back through Porlock it lies at your feet as you drive down into the valley below, and there appeared to be a fair sprinkling of thatched cottages. At one part of the road at Porlock an apple tree with fruit on it hung across the road, so that any person on the coach could easily pick the apples. A few miles out of Minehead there are some workmen's allotments, and I saw on them three little thatched stacks of grain.

Before getting to Minehead it got dark, and we had to stop for the guard to light the three large coach lamps. We drove right down The Avenue to the station before any one got down, arriving at 8.15pm. The trip there and back is forty two miles, and a very enjoyable one it is.

The horse-drawn vehicles certainly helped to open up the charms of Exmoor to a wider public. A drive behind a pair of horses on a fine summer's day, at a pace which enabled the views to be fully appreciated, must have been a joy. The four-in-hand and stagecoach may have passed into history but we have in our vocabulary reminders of their colourful existence. For example, we travel in railway 'carriages' and we buy our tickets at a 'booking office' from a 'booking clerk', although our seats are no longer registered in the 'book'. The name 'guard' belongs to the days when the stagecoach guard was required to protect the lives of the passengers.

An excursion party and G.R. Carpenter's coach, 'Tally Ho!' Coach horses were hard worked and this shows in the condition of one of the leading horses. (BA)

Part Three
THE MOTOR AGE

The Minehead Area in the 1920s

While many English seaside resorts came into being as a result of geographic advantage and historic events, other factors influenced their future development and popularity.

Following the First World War the overriding influences were the introduction of paid holidays for the working classes and a railway network offering relatively cheap and convenient travel to virtually all parts of the country. The day of the British seaside holiday had arrived and resorts reacted by providing a range of affordable accommodation and a variety of entertainments. Minehead was not going to miss out and, what is more, the opportunity was there to take advantage of the beauty of the surrounding countryside. This was exploited to the full by rapidly developing local motor-coach businesses.

Minehead was then an altogether different type of resort than it is today. The town was still largely catering for the hunting, walking and riding fraternity but it became increasingly popular for what became known as 'bucket and spade' holidays.

The Avenue, with its elegant buildings and mature trees, provided the main approach to the sea front. The Square, complete with the single frontage of Floyd's store on one side and the elegant aspect of the Plume of Feathers Hotel on another, was a focal point for assemblies of all descriptions.

The Avenue, Minehead, in the 1930s, fronted by well proportioned hotels, private residences and business premises. During the motor coach age Scarlet Pimpernel, Blue Motors and Western National all had their main offices in the street. Note the steep camber on the carriageway, to shed the water and cleanse the road before the days of tarmacadam. (PC)

As for life in the town, a real feeling is obtained from a description by Sidney Whitehead and published in an issue of the *Exmoor Review*:

We first went to Minehead in 1922 or 1923, by train, and I don't think I've missed a year since, except during the last war. Next year we went by car, a Model T Ford. We used to stay in Irnham Road, and with luck would be there when the fun fair arrived. I can still recall the thrill of seeing the steam traction engines arriving, with a string of trailers behind them. No beach for me that day. There was a tannery where the Regal Cinema is now, and it gave off some strange odours. There was however a little cinema in Bancks Street. No Blenheim Gardens then, just a field with a hedge along the side of the road, and cows grazing.

The harbour was still quite busy in the 1920s and 1930s. All the coal for the gas works came by sea. A steam crane used to unload it in big iron buckets and tip it into carts, later lorries. Sailing boats took pit props over to South Wales. The last was the 'Emma Louise'. I saw one of the steam boats sucked out dry by the tide. The hawsers could not hold her. They cleared everyone from the harbour. When the rope snapped, it coiled

right up in the air and sounded as if a gun had gone off. The pier was taken down in the war to prevent a landing but has never been put back. Campbell's steamers used to call daily. Folks came over from South Wales. There was even a little railway along the pier for moving the luggage. The crossing could be rough, and passengers arrived in various shades of green. Sometimes they had to hose the decks down before anyone was allowed on board again.

The best hotel was the 'Metropole'. Guests could be seen coming out after dinner, all in evening dress, for a stroll. The Indian Princes used to stay there when playing polo at Dunster. The hotel had a lift and you could watch it going up and down. There was a band stand in Jubilee Gardens, where Ivy Benson and her girls used to play; and a concert party in the old Gaiety Theatre. Chars-a-banc would line up on the sea front opposite the Beach Hotel. I can remember some of the names, 'Lorna Doone', 'Mascot', 'Scarlet Pimpernel', 'Pride of the Moors'. American Reo chassis were favoured because they had powerful engines, and Italian Lancias as they had four wheel brakes. Some were good going up hills, some coming down!

A Blue Motors open charabanc waits on the Minehead hackney carriage stand on the sea front, thronged with holidaymakers in deckchairs. (PC)

Contemporary local guides give a further glimpse, particularly from the traveller's point of view. For example:

The Exmoor area embraces the north-western part of Somerset, overlapping into North Devon, and is bounded to the north by the Bristol Channel. A more lovely part of England for a holiday visit it would hardly be possible to conceive. The principal towns are Minehead, Dunster, Dulverton, Porlock and Lynton, of which the former is the largest.

From London, Minehead, the capital of the seaside of West Somerset, is one hundred and sixty eight miles distant. Return fares from Paddington are seventy shillings (£3.10s.0d.) First Class; two guineas (£2.2s.0d.) Third Class.

The Great Western route from Paddington as far as Taunton is probably familiar to everyone who knows the West of England.

At the latter station travellers from London would alight and be joined by those arriving from the Midlands, the North of England and South Wales. The extract continues:

The countrified little line to Watchet and Minehead is not perhaps so well known. The trains usually start from a side platform at Taunton and the run of twenty miles along the single line is a pleasant foretaste of the rich

and varied scenery at its termination. On the right the Quantock Hills, whose rounded outlines become very familiar during a visit to Minehead, are visible for the whole distance, so that to enjoy the best views it is better to take a seat on the right hand side of the carriage, facing the engine.

At Watchet the line reaches the coast, but after passing St Decuman's Church, plunges inland again for Washford. Soon after passing that station the line runs once more close to the sea, along whose bordering marshes it goes past Blue Anchor. Then comes Dunster, with a fleeting glimpse of its castle overlooking the heavily wooded hollow where the town lies.

For those alighting here, GWR publicity waxed lyrical about the mile-long walk from the station to Dunster village: 'Down a shady field-fringed road, fragrant with meadowsweet. Then a few scattered cottages, quaint beyond words; a sharp turn, and one stands at the head of Dunster street, most perfect street man ever gazed upon.' Back on the train leaving Dunster station, 'a few minutes later the terminus at Minehead is reached'.

This was one way of railway approach. But for those visiting Minehead from the West of England, there was a road route offering manifold attractions:

Minehead station yard in the 1920s. Minehead was an important railhead, serving a wide area of Exmoor, and a taxi, saloon buses for Lynmouth and Porlock Weir, two open charabancs and a small horse-drawn omnibus await passengers. (AM)

From Barnstaple a light railway runs to Lynton, whence in summer the 'Lorna Doone' motor coach leaves in the morning in connection with the Great Western Railway at Minehead. This drive crosses the highest part of Exmoor by a road from 1200 to 1400 feet above the sea, skirting in many parts the precipitous coast-line. After the steep hill from Lynmouth up to Countisbury has been mounted, the road lies for some eight miles over heather covered uplands above Brendon, Oare and the Doone Valley. Then by an appallingly steep descent, three miles in length, the coach descends into Porlock vale, whence there remains a comparatively level and lowland course of six miles to Minehead.

Well-appointed steamboats also called at Minehead, where a pier was completed in 1901. This served a useful purpose in opening up communications with the Welsh coast, 'affording an opportunity for the Cardiff and Bristol steamers, in their progress up and down the Channel, to call at nearly all states of the tide'. Emerging from the shelter of North Hill, the pier also made an excellent promenade, affording bracing breezes at the extremity. A little trolley for carrying luggage to and from the steamers ran on a rail up the centre.

The narrow-gauge Lynton and Barnstaple Railway was picturesque but slow. It succumbed to road competition in 1935. (PC)

Minehead was thus approachable from several directions and visitors to the town could come and go by different routes.

The delightful situation of Minehead and the natural beauty of its surroundings made it an ideal holiday resort for many people. Hotels and boarding houses sought to attract holidaymakers with inducements such as: 'One minute from the sea, modern sanitation, hot and cold running water in all rooms, good cuisine, separate tables, moderate tariff', all designed to make individual establishments stand out from the multitude.

For those who liked a lively holiday there were the sands and the gaiety of daily entertainments. Touring theatrical companies and concert parties played at the Queen's Hall and orchestral and pierrot performances were given on the promenade during the season. From 1934 the Regal, in The Avenue, catered for film-goers and dancers. For those who sought peace and beauty there was the glorious hinterland, with woods, picturesque villages and, of course, Exmoor, an area of astonishing beauty and the land of Lorna Doone and the home of wild red deer.

Whether coming for a family holiday at the seaside or a more leisurely look at nature, visitors usually wished to spend some time seeing the locality. In those days when private car ownership was very much the exception, the means of reaching beauty spots and places of interest was public transport.

Throughout the summer excursions ran daily to all places of interest in the locality and farther afield. The ubiquitous motor coach could be seen on the winding moorland roads, wending its way to Dunkery Beacon, the highest

The Avenue and Parade, Minehead, with coaches ready for local excursions. The then newly built Regal Cinema can be seen in the background and opposite it a Scarlet Pimpernel coach waits outside the Hawkins Brothers' booking office. (MS)

point on Exmoor, and to Malmsmead, the gateway to the Doone Valley. Longer journeys were made as far as Cheddar, Glastonbury, Wells, Exeter, Ilfracombe and Clovelly.

The hunting of deer is a feature of the area. The season begins at the end of July, with the opening meet at Cloutsham. It continues to the second week in October, with an interval until Christmas; hind-hunting then is continued up to the end of March, finishing with a week's stag-hunting in April. Minehead was a good centre for the meets and the motor-coach proprietors ran trips from the town during the hunting season, these helping to extend the season and bringing welcome extra revenue.

In addition to the excursion coaches, regular motor services served the district. Twice daily during the season, at about 9.30am, after the arrival of the first train at Minehead, and at about 4.30pm, after the arrival of the train which left Paddington at about one o'clock, a powerful motor coach left Minehead Great Western Railway Station for the grand ride of twenty miles to Lynton. It was one of the most famous coach rides in the Kingdom and not until 1920 did the all-conquering motor supersede the more picturesque horse-drawn vehicles on this route.

'With the Devon and Somerset', from a painting by G.D. Armour. Sailor: 'I don't know much about that kind of navigation, but it looks to me as 'ow the capting might be leaving the ship pretty soon.' (MH)

Motor omnibuses ran daily throughout the year from Minehead to Porlock Weir and back. Another useful daily service was that eastward from Minehead via Dunster and Williton to Bridgwater, providing excellent facilities for visiting the beautiful Quantock Hills. Dulverton, too, could be reached from Minehead by motor, the drive being a very fine one. Motor buses linked Minehead, Alcombe and Dunster daily, and various places in the district were served regularly on certain days of the week. The steamers carried excursionists from Minehead pier, visiting Ilfracombe, Clovelly, Lundy Island and Weston-super-Mare.

Thus, the 1920s visitor to the capital of the seaboard of Exmoor – Minehead – had a wide choice of public transport and an opportunity to see much of the

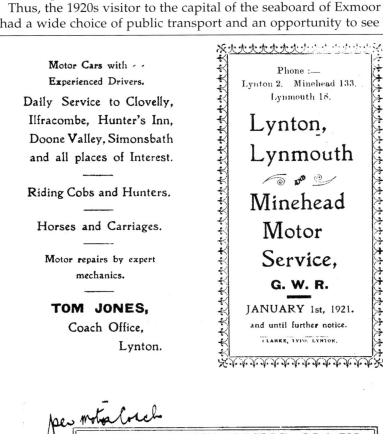

Motor Cars with · ·
Experienced Drivers.

Daily Service to Clovelly,
Ilfracombe, Hunter's Inn,
Doone Valley, Simonsbath
and all places of Interest.

Riding Cobs and Hunters.

Horses and Carriages.

Motor repairs by expert
mechanics.

TOM JONES,
Coach Office,
Lynton.

Phone :—
Lynton 2. Minehead 133.
Lynmouth 16.

Lynton, Lynmouth
Minehead Motor Service,
G. W. R.

JANUARY 1st, 1921.
and until further notice.

CLARKE, TYPO. LYNTON.

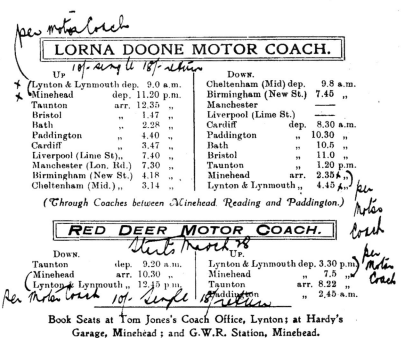

LORNA DOONE MOTOR COACH.

Up			Down.		
(Lynton & Lynmouth	dep.	9.0 a.m.	Cheltenham (Mid)	dep.	9.8 a.m.
Minehead	dep.	11.20 p.m.	Birmingham (New St.)		7.45 ,,
Taunton	arr.	12.35 ,,	Manchester		—
Bristol	,,	1.47 ,,	Liverpool (Lime St.)		—
Bath	,,	2.28 ,,	Cardiff	dep.	8.30 a.m.
Paddington	,,	4.40 ,,	Paddington	,,	10.30 ,,
Cardiff	,,	3.47 ,,	Bath	,,	10.5 ,,
Liverpool (Lime St.)	,,	7.40 ,,	Bristol	,,	11.0 ,,
Manchester (Lon. Rd.)	,,	7.30 ,,	Taunton	,,	1.20 p.m.
Birmingham (New St.)	,,	4.18 ,,	Minehead	arr.	2.35 ,,
Cheltenham (Mid.)	,,	3.14 ,,	Lynton & Lynmouth	,,	4.45 ,,

(Through Coaches between Minehead, Reading and Paddington.)

RED DEER MOTOR COACH.

Down.			Up.		
Taunton	dep.	9.20 a.m.	Lynton & Lynmouth	dep.	3.30 p.m.
Minehead	arr.	10.30 ,,	Minehead	,,	7.5 ,,
Lynton & Lynmouth	,,	12.45 p.m.	Taunton	arr.	8.22 ,,
			Paddington	,,	2.45 a.m.

Book Seats at Tom Jones's Coach Office, Lynton ; at Hardy's
Garage, Minehead ; and G.W.R. Station, Minehead.

Passengers' Luggage conveyed as per Railway Company's Regulations.

wonderful scenery of the district from motor buses and coaches whose standards of reliability and comfort steadily improved throughout the decade. In addition, careful and experienced local drivers were in charge on roads which held many terrors for the inexperienced or nervous motorist. Porlock and Countisbury gave this part of England a certain notoriety in the matter of hills. The surface of the main roads was generally reasonable but by-roads could be untarred, with loose surfaces which were apt to be rather dangerous in certain circumstances. As a contemporary guide advises visitors:

> A feature of some of the subsidiary lanes is that they pass through the middle of farmyards, so that in addition to negotiating the inevitable fowls, ducks, geese and pigs, one has to be prepared to find the way out again – all of which is a very enjoyable holiday experience, providing, of course, you have a knowledgeable local chauffeur!

Motor Services in the Minehead Area

In the early days of motoring the services of a knowledgeable local chauffeur was highly desirable. In an area where potential disaster lurked on every hill and at each bend, confidence in the driver and his ability to control the machine was essential if full enjoyment was to be obtained from any excursion.

The early motor coaches were primitive and unreliable and the operators required perserverance and ingenuity, courage and resolve in full measure. Motors were difficult to start and, once started, not easy to stop. It was said that more time was spent tinkering than driving. After dark drivers had to rely on flickering oil lamps to light their way. Most roads were quite unsuitable and the loose surfaces created clouds of dust in summer, enveloping the vehicle and blinding the driver. In winter they would be rutted and muddy, making progress difficult. The twists and gradients on the roads around Exmoor added to the problems.

For the first passengers there was small comfort. Solid tyres and a distinct lack of springs gave a hard, jolting ride and there was little protection from the wind and rain. Added to this was the need to walk up the steepest hills and to push the vehicle when the gradient was beyond its climbing capabilities. Many of the pioneering vehicles were wagonettes. Although they had a chassis and engine designed for carrying up to four passengers, they were fitted with a larger body able to accommodate perhaps fourteen. Expecting a six-horsepower engine to pull that number of passengers (and sometimes their luggage as well) up the steep hills of North Devon and West Somerset often led to disappointment and failure. In spite of the noise, dust, discomfort and cold, people wanted to ride in motor coaches and some entrepreneurs seized the opportunity to carry them.

As ever, the challenge of the new appealed to those of a pioneering spirit and people from many different trades tried their hand at motorised passenger transport. Some were already carrying people in horse-drawn carriages and merely changed the mode of traction. Others were new to the transport industry but saw the commercial possibilities of the motor vehicle. Some prospered; others were beaten by high repair costs or the intense competition. Those that survived saw improvements in design that enabled the motor coach to match the private car for comfort. The coach outing or excursion was eagerly anticipated, then greatly enjoyed and talked about for long after. Motor bus services became part of everyday life and virtually every settlement of any size around Exmoor was served at least once a week.

A bus journey was a friendly, social occasion, allowing plenty of time to exchange the latest gossip. As one former passenger recalled: 'We didn't have a car but a bus ride was affordable and still a treat. There were lovely leather and cloth seats and the conductor with his ticket-clipping machine and warm smile,

This 1921 Daimler 26-seater bus (YA1591) was described by its owners, the Hardy Central Garage Company of Minehead, as a 'Luxurious Saloon Motor Bus fitted with every modern convenience'. It was used on the Bridgwater route. (RG)

ever friendly and helpful.' The driver and conductor knew their regulars well, and it is said that a few enterprising conductors carried a gun with them and considered a route a bad one if it did not provide a rabbit or two for the pot.

Motor traction is thought to have first been used in the Minehead area in 1909, by Arthur Surridge. It was a relatively short-lived experiment. The Surridge family were in business before the end of the nineteenth century and by 1897 John Surridge was a jobmaster with livery stables in Bampton Street. He hired out horses and carriages of all descriptions and ran trips over Exmoor. A relative of his, Arthur Surridge, traded as a draper from a shop in Friday Street. He seems to have been interested in motor traction, for he developed the Minehead Motor and Engineering Works in Alcombe. In April 1909 he put on the road a Wolseley wagonette capable of carrying fourteen passengers. The body was light varnished and the wheels were painted red, making it a smart turn-out. The chassis was that of a private motor car and, given the state of the roads in the Minehead area at the time and the hilly nature of the terrain, the vehicle would have been severely challenged when fully loaded. It ran for two years until, in the first few days of 1911, it was taken off the road and the number assigned to a car belonging to a Mr Potter.

From then until the end of the 1914–18 war Arthur Surridge seems to have concentrated on hiring out open and closed motor cars and motor engineering. In the 1920s, with somewhat improved roads and more powerful vehicles available, he entered the charabanc trade and established a Booking Office at No. 8, The Avenue. Using the title 'Pride of the Moors', he ran Napier open vehicles on daily trips over Exmoor and to other places of interest, picking up passengers at the office and at his garage at Alcombe. At the latter motor repairs of every description were undertaken and tyres, petrol and accessories stocked.

By 1931 the coach fleet consisted of four all-weather coaches, which ventured as far afield as Sidmouth, Weston-super-Mare, Bournemouth, Weymouth and Bristol. In addition there was an attempt to run a regular motor bus service between Minehead, Wheddon Cross, Winsford and Exford but permission was refused.

In 1934 Arthur Surridge sold out to Herbert Stone of Bicknoller. A man of many parts, he traded a dealer in coal, cement and logs, he was a motor haulier and motor-car proprietor, owned the Cosy Cinema, Watchet, and until the early 1930s ran the Relion Bus Service. After selling this to Thomas Motors of Taunton, he continued to operate coach tours from Watchet. Between 1934 and 1937 he also ran the former Surridge excursions from Minehead but then apparently got into difficulties and his licences were auctioned. Mr Stone failed in his attempt to buy them back and they passed to Tom Heard and Son of Timberscombe.

Although Arthur Surridge can possibly claim to be the first to run a motor wagonette locally, the man who really pioneered the motor bus and charabanc trade in Minehead was James Hardy. Just before the First World War Hardy purchased the business of Harold Langdon of Minehead, jobmaster, carriage hirer and proprietor of the 'Red Deer' coach which ran between Minehead station and Lynmouth. It would appear that his intention was to change over to motor traction and develop bus services and charabanc tours around the locality and further afield. The former Langdon stables were converted into the Central Garage. The garage held an agency for the Ford Motor Company, and from April 1914 had a 20-horsepower Ford with a torpedo body as a hire car.

Hardy's purchase of a Napier charabanc in 1915 saw the inauguration of the 'Silver Streak' motor tours and an omnibus of the same make, bought in April 1916, was used to start a motor bus service between Minehead, Porlock and Porlock Weir. The latter seemingly displaced Goddard's horse-bus service. The road beyond Porlock to Lynmouth was not considered suitable for use by motors, being 'as steep as the side of a house'. Therefore, the 'Red Deer', which ran in conjunction with the 'Lorna Doone' coach from Lynton, continued to use horse traction.

From Minehead coaches generally carried passengers travelling beyond Porlock, local traffic being catered for by the Anchor Hotel bus which ran between Minehead and Porlock Weir. The horse-drawn bus, seen here, gave way to Hardy's motor omnibus in 1916.

Later in 1916, with the war dragging on, James Hardy sold the Porlock Weir service, together with a Napier bus, to a local syndicate, the Porlock Weir, Porlock and Minehead Motor Service Company.

It was not until after the Armistice that Mr Hardy was able to expand his business. This he did with a will. In 1919 he bought Delauney Belleville, Austin, Karrier and Albion charabancs and the 'Silver Streak' tours were re-started and expanded. Over the next few years the firm undertook not only the popular local excursions but some ambitious trips to distant places, given the state of the roads and unreliability of early vehicles.

Locally, there were daily trips to Lynmouth and the Doone Valley and a Special Circular Tour through the heart of Exmoor, via Porlock Vale, Hawkcombe Head and Chetsford Water to Exford for tea. The latter left Minehead at 2.15pm, fare ten shillings and sixpence. An afternoon run over Dunkery, allowing time at Horner for tea, cost five shillings. Every Monday and Thursday a charabanc would leave at 9.30am for another Circular Tour over Exmoor to Tarr Steps, the forward journey being through Porlock to Lynmouth, where there was a two-hour stay. Then on via Simonsbath and Tarr Steps (half an hour's

The magnificent West Front of Exeter Cathedral with Hardy's 'Silver Streak' charabanc on an excursion from Minehead. (PC)

stop), continuing along the Barle Valley to Dulverton. After an hour in this pleasant little town the homeward journey was through Timberscombe and Dunster. The tour was claimed to be 'unsurpassed in England, embracing magnificent Moorland, Coast, River and Alpine Scenery and passing through nearly the whole of the Hunting ground of the famous Devon and Somerset Staghounds (Return fare: fifteen shillings)'.

The more distant destinations included Weymouth, Cheddar, an all-day trip to Bournemouth and 'the Finest Circular Tour in the West of England – from the Bristol Channel to the English Channel', covering Taunton, Bridport, Lyme Regis, Sidmouth and Exeter.

The business was converted into a limited liability company, Hardy Central Garage Company Ltd, the directors of which were James Hardy and two Bristol businessmen. Its activities included motor coach tours and private party outings, bus services, heavy and light haulage contracting, furniture removing, motor engineering, car sales and the hiring out of open and closed cars.

Vehicle purchases continued and motor bus services were inaugurated from Minehead to Dunster, Exford, Dulverton and Luxborough. In the company's publicity each route was described fully. The Exford route description read:

> A climb of over 1000 feet, revealing a glimpse of the further vastness of Exmoor, is involved on this journey. The way lies through Dunster, where the scene of an old-fashioned street in an old-fashioned town, dominated by its Historical Castle, makes an unfading impression on all who behold it; then onward through the pleasant valley which winds southwards by Timberscombe until the long ascent to Wheddon Cross is reached and passing through Luckwell Bridge we see Dunkery to our right, rising to a height of 1700 feet. We then reach Exford, the home of the Hounds and Huntsmen of the Devon and Somerset Stag-hunt.

This route was not just intended for visitors. On the third Monday in each Month (Minehead Auction Day) a special service was run for farmers and other moor-dwellers wishing to go into town for the market.

It had been intended to continue some journeys through from Exford to Dulverton but the Rural District Council considered the roads unsuitable and refused permission. The company then stated they would run a direct service from Minehead to Dulverton and as this route lay over main roads, no objection was raised. Polo at Dunster Lawns drew crowds and on match days a bus left the Central Garage, Minehead, at 2.30pm. On the Luxborough service

a combined bus and cinema ticket was issued on Saturdays, holders being entitled to entry to the Cosy Cinema as well as a ride in and out of Minehead.

The advent of more powerful vehicles permitted Hardy and Tom Jones to motorise the Minehead–Lynmouth service from 1920. Hardy's vehicle left Minehead at 10.45am, reaching Lynmouth at 12.45pm, returning at 3pm via Brendon and the Doone Valley to arrive Minehead at 6.15pm. Tom Jones' chara-banc left Lynton and Lynmouth in the morning and returned from Minehead in the afternoon, meeting the principal trains to and from London. The desirabil-ity of providing for luggage on this service led to the fitting of 'a capacious luggage locker fitted at the rear of the vehicle'. This was a large box slung under the chassis and it was the subject of comment from the large crowd which gath-ered to see it tackle Porlock Hill on Good Friday, 1920. One journalist from the trade press thought the arrangement 'not pleasing to look at and liable to make the car skid on grease'. The necessity for very careful driving was also noted.

The passing of the old established and much loved horse-drawn coaches caused sadness. As noted at the time:

> The ubiquitous motor, as was inevitable, has driven the grand old Lynton, Lynmouth and Minehead stagecoach off the road. The pride of North Devon and West Somerset, its departure is viewed with deepest regret by many visitors and residents along its route. At Lynmouth and Minehead its arrivals and departures were events of the day and in all the intervening villages its passage was viewed with interest, the guard's horn bringing good housewives to the door. But in these utilitarian times sentiment finds no place. People are in a hurry in holiday-keeping as in business. So the three and a half hour coach journey is ... superseded by that of a motor charabanc taking just half the time.

For a time the motors retained the names of the stagecoaches: 'Red Deer' and 'Lorna Doone'.

However, the passing of the horses did not mean that the route lost any of its popularity, as this quote from the local press in 1921 shows: 'The splendidly organised service of Messrs Hardy, in conjunction with Tom Jones, ensures the utmost prospect to passengers and goods and for the former the most comfort-able and safest travelling.' On one day in August of that year 150 passengers with luggage were taken by these well-appointed motors to Minehead and a similar number of new arrivals brought back. 'It is now part of the mornings doings to watch these powerful machines ascend the famous Countisbury and Porlock Hills,' the newspaper stated.

On Sundays Hardy's motor ran through to Taunton station, there being no

1921 Leyland advertisement featuring the vehicle used on the Minehead–Lynmouth route. (See also page 12.)

DESCENDING TO LYNMOUTH.

The Motor Coach 'Lorna Doone' replaced the four-in-hand of the same name on the route to Minehead. Here it descends Countisbury Hill to Lynmouth and the large luggage locker at the rear can clearly be seen. The wall on the right, separating the road from a sheer drop to the sea, was built as traffic increased. (MS)

Schoolchildren watch as efforts are made to retrieve a motor bus that has come to grief on the Minehead and Dunster route. (KA)

trains on the Minehead branch on that day. Leaving Lynmouth at 1pm, Minehead at 2.30pm, it connected with the Bristol and London up trains. The return journey left the Great Western Railway Hotel yard after the arrival of the 5.29pm down train, running as far as Lynton.

During 1921 more new buses were bought. Hardy advertised: 'Luxurious Saloon Motor Buses fitted with every modern convenience, including Electric Light and Super Resilient Tyres, which give the greatest amount of comfort without the risk of puncture'. These were available at all times for 'Football, Cricket, Wedding and Picnic Parties'.

A service was inaugurated between Minehead and Bridgwater, described by the operators as 'passing through some very fine scenery'. Holford Glen, at the foot of the Quantock Hills, was said to be a pleasant half-day's excursion or the journey could be extended to Bridgwater, 'the birthplace of Admiral Blake'. Expansion continued unabated and, by a mixture of acquisitions and the introduction of new services, the company grew to cover a wide area of West Somerset, North Devon and North Cornwall. Among the businesses taken over were Tom Jones of Lynton and Colwill's of Ilfracombe. Following the latter purchase the firm became known as Hardy-Colwill's.

Running the early vehicles over the challenging terrain, through a sparsely populated countryside, was never easy nor particularly profitable. Therefore, in 1927, the directors must have been glad to negotiate the sale of the business to the National Omnibus and Transport Company Ltd for the then considerable sum of £48,500.

One other Minehead firm ran a motor charabanc before the First World War. William Staddon had started life as a cabinet-maker but at the turn of the century became a proprietor of horse-drawn carriages and brakes and specialised in taking visitors for trips over the moor. William and his sons placed a Karrier motor charabanc on the road at the end of May 1914 and this is reputed to have been the first passenger vehicle to climb the notorious Porlock Hill, with its one-in-four gradient. It did so among clouds of exhaust smoke while a man walked beside it carrying skids to place under the wheels should the vehicle fail to negotiate the loose surface and sharp bends. Due to wartime restrictions the Karrier was withdrawn from passenger service in July 1915 and the firm did not re-enter the charabanc business but concentrated on motor engineering at their Bampton Street premises for many years thereafter.

When Staddon's of Minehead bought a new Karrier charabanc in 1914, just before the outbreak of the Great War, the family went for a trip over Exmoor. Their vehicle thus became the first local charabanc to climb Porlock Hill. The events of the day, pictured below, were photographed by Alfred Vowles.

Ascending Porlock Hill in a cloud of dust. One passenger anxiously looks over the side while a man walks behind ready to put a block under the wheels should the motor fail. (KA/KS)

A stop at the Ship Inn, Porlock (KA/KS)

Staddon's motor meets the Lynton to Minehead coach on the moors between Porlock and Countisbury. (KA/KS)

Passing through Porlock Parks (KA/KS)

The first local charabanc to climb Porlock Hill meets the military on horseback. (KA/KS)

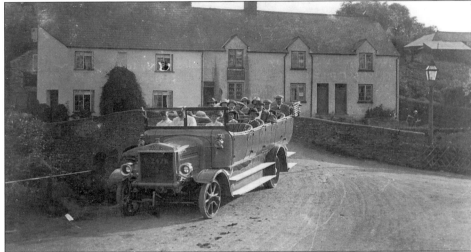

The tour party stops in Exford. (MS/KS)

On the bridge, Dulverton. (MS/KS)

The syndicate who bought James Hardy's Minehead and Porlock Weir motor bus service formed a limited company with the lengthy title of The Porlock Weir, Porlock and Minehead Motor Service Company Ltd. From 1920 the firm expanded, running excursions from Minehead and Porlock to places in the locality, as well as private party outings. Early chars-a-banc carried the names 'Empress', 'Queen of the West' and 'Princess' but then the title 'Blue Motors' was adopted for the whole fleet, reflecting the livery used.

During the 1930s streamlined luxury observation coaches of Dennis, Albion and Leyland manufacture were owned, with the company matching every

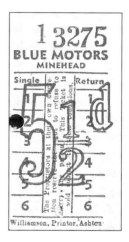

The streamlined look was characteristic of the modern 1930s motor coach. This Blue Motors observation coach had glass panels in the roof and the dorsal fin at the rear vented air into the saloon. (ABC)

move of their main excursion competitor, Scarlet Pimpernel, including buying very similar vehicles. Blue Motors expanded by the acquisition of several small operators, taking over F. Harrison, Bryant Brothers and G. Cann.

During World War Two activities were restricted and staff shortages led to women being employed as conductresses on the Porlock Weir bus service. The post-war years brought a boom time, with most people dependent on public transport. The excursion programme, popular with visitors to the Somerset coast, resumed and holiday tours to Scotland, Wales, the Lake District and Blackpool were introduced. At the peak of the summer season the coach fleet was hard pressed to cope with demand. Times on the bus service to Porlock Weir had been co-ordinated with those of Western National (as successors to Eli Ford) since the 1930s and from 1946 each operator accepted tickets issued by the other. This joint operation continued until 1953, when Blue Motors sold their share of the route to the National company. The coaching activities continued until the following year, when the company merged with their main rivals, Hawkins Brothers, proprietors of the Scarlet Pimpernel Coaches, to form Scarlet and Blue Motor Coaches Ltd.

Full details of the history of the Porlock Blue company can be found in *The Blue Motors Remembered*, by Roy H. Lee (Roadmaster Publishing, 1994).

The 1920s brought many new entrants into the motor bus and charabanc trade. Some replaced their horse-drawn carriages with motor charabancs; others started new businesses. Some local hotel and boarding-house proprietors ran their own motor trips, thus widening the services offered to their guests and providing additional income for a seasonal business.

Building bodies for the new motor charabancs also provided work locally, and in the early years firms such as Williams and Son of Friday Street, Minehead, produced some fine examples. The firm had started by building to order horse-drawn carriages and undertaking repairs, painting, trimming and leatherwork of every description. They turned to building charabanc coachwork but, by the end of the decade charabancs had become obsolete. By 1929 they had been replaced by 'all-weather' coaches, pneumatic-tyred vehicles with enclosed saloon bodies and a quality of finish equal to the finest private cars of the day. Passengers were no longer open to the elements, although sliding roof panels were particularly popular in the Westcountry, coaches thus fitted being known as 'sun-saloons'. Specialist national coachbuilders went into mass production and the products of the small local body shops were no longer needed by operators who were now not charabanc proprietors but motor-coach owners.

As the number of vehicles competing for the custom of visitors wishing to take a motor tour increased, it became necessary for operators to find some

Blue Motors' AEC bus HYB676, driven by Tom Bowden or his son Ernie, regularly covered the route between Minehead and Porlock Weir for Blue Motors. (ABC)

means of differentiating their service from the others. Everyone offered similar trips to the main points of interest and beauty spots on Exmoor, so some proprietors chose to highlight the colours of their charabancs. Silver-grey, blue, scarlet, yellow and green coaches caught the eye. Others looked for a name that either created an impression or evoked local stories: 'Pride of the Moors', 'Lorna Doone', 'Mascot Safety', 'Swift' and 'Red Deer'.

To attract the attention of passers-by and to ensure that no opportunity was lost to take bookings, touts would stand on the pavements of the resort. They could make even the most mundane drive sound as though it was a journey not to be missed on any account, although sometimes enthusiasm did get in the way of accuracy.

'Good morning sir, madam,' they might begin. 'What a lovely day for a drive. I am sure on a beautiful morning such as this you would not wish to miss seeing Exmoor at its loveliest. You can ride in the most comfortable, reliable and up-to-date coach in the area, with the finest driver in the county, see places more beautiful than you could ever imagine, have the best cream tea in the Westcountry and be back in time for dinner. A tour to delight you both and only seven shillings each. Step this way and we will book your seats.'

And before they knew it, 'sir' and 'madam', who a few minutes earlier had

The traditional way of attracting excursion passengers. Frank Harrison, a local charabanc proprietor, attempts to sell a trip to a passer-by. Behind him, blackboards beside the waiting coaches advertise the excursions on offer. (AM)

no intention of doing other than strolling along the sea front, were ensconced in a nearby charabanc with a glazed look in their eyes, ready to start a tour.

One firm which reflected the progress from horses and the link with accommodation was Hobbs and Co. The firm originated in the days of horse traction as jobmasters and livery stable keepers, funeral furnishers, furniture removers and haulage contractors. Carriages of all description were available for hire at their premises at Allenhayes in The Avenue and at the Beach Hotel Stables. During the 1920s the horse-drawn charabancs used on local excursions from The Avenue and sea front were gradually replaced by the Lorna Doone Motor Coaches. As well as continuing with the traditional destinations, such as Dunkery, Horner Woods, Porlock Weir and the Doone Valley, the motor vehicles travelled farther afield, reaching Glastonbury, Wells, and Cheddar.

At Allenhayes accommodation was available, either on full-board terms or by renting an apartment, and guests could avail themselves of trips in the Lorna Doone Coaches. For those wishing to take private trips, open and closed motor cars with experienced drivers were available for hire while, for motorists, there were private lock-ups at Hobbs' motor garage in Mart Road. The fleet of motor coaches numbered four by the Spring of 1936 when the coaching business was sold to Hawkins Brothers, the Hobbs family continuing with their garage and taxi enterprises.

The Plume of Feathers Hotel, proprietor Henry Redvers Chidgey, was situated in the town and was separated from the railway station by the length of The Avenue. For the convenience of guests the Hotel Motor Bus met all trains at Minehead station and conveyed passengers and their luggage to and fro. Operations commenced in 1921 and ceased in 1931.

Mr F.H. Harrison and his wife let apartments at Stargroves, The Quay, to visitors. In addition, Frank Harrison ran excursions starting from the Bungalow Café on the sea front. At first he used a large Overland car, carrying parties of

(Above left) The Hobbs family business originated with horse traction but after the First World War they turned to motors. Here, Maurice Hobbs is at the wheel of his Arrol-Johnson hire car in 1921. (RH)

(Above right) Hobbs' 'Lorna Doone' motor coach ready for a day's work. The side screens gave passengers some protection from the wind, but rain is evidently not expected, as the roof is open. (RH)

(Left) Hobbs' Dennis coach outside Allenhayes, on the corner of The Avenue and Glenmore Road, Minehead, in the late 1920s. (RH)

up to six people, but later he bought from Blue Motors a fourteen-seater Crossley charabanc which was repainted green and named 'The Swift'. Apart from the usual trips over Exmoor, a circular tour of the Brendon Hills ran until operations ceased in the 1930s.

The use of taxis or hire cars to convey small parties of visitors around the area sometimes led to the introduction of a charabanc service. One example of this was Mr Walter Adams, who lived at Penryn in Irnham Road. Before the

The ascent and descent of Porlock Hill, with steep gradients and hairpin bends, was a memorable experience for visitors to Exmoor. The camera of Sidney Whitehead caught a selection of early vehicles struggling up or being eased down the dreaded hill. (SW)

(Above)   An Albion of Blue Motors goes down the hill as a photographer with a Box Brownie type camera awaits another photo opportunity.
(Right)   Blue Motors Albion YD7169 at full throttle round an upward bend

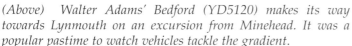

(Above)   Walter Adams' Bedford (YD5120) makes its way towards Lynmouth on an excursion from Minehead. It was a popular pastime to watch vehicles tackle the gradient.

(Right)   A Blue Motors Albion (YB5915) edges round the corner as a saloon car, with rear rack well loaded with luggage, crawls up.

(Bottom right) A 1929 Daimler luxury touring coach (UW4105), spare wheel mounted on the running board, brings a party from London down the hill towards Porlock and Minehead.

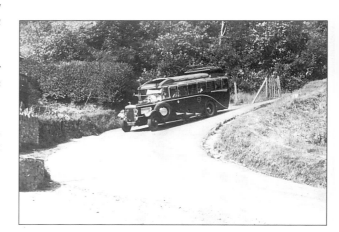

Great War he was in partnership with a Mr Passmore as a jobmaster, trading from the Plume of Feathers yard. By 1922 he alone was trading from the Market House Lane Garage, from where open and closed cars were available for hire. To cater for larger parties, a motor coach was purchased and this plied for hire from the stand on the sea front, competing with other operators, but offering trips to Dartmoor, South Devon and Dorset as well as the usual Exmoor and Cheddar destinations. During the stag-hunting season the coach ran to all meets and, in winter, there were trips to Bristol for football matches and pantomimes. The tours were suspended early in the Second World War and the coach sold to Mr Street, owner of the Quantock Coach Service, Watchet. In the post-war years Mr Adams ran a taxi service in Minehead.

George Cann of Victoria Terrace, Alcombe, began running charabanc trips from Minehead sea front to Exmoor, Clovelly, Cheddar, Sidmouth, Ilfracombe and Exeter in the mid-1920s. He owned two coaches and also ran to Barnstaple Fair (the premier event in North Devon, attracting thousands to 'Barum' every September), to Bampton Fair, and Bridgwater for both the annual fair and the town's renowned carnival. Mr Cann sold out to Blue Motors in 1937.

The firm of Bryant Brothers in Bampton Street traded as furniture removers and charabanc proprietors, built and repaired motor bodies and traded as carpenters and joiners, from premises in Summerland Avenue. They ran summer excursions to a number of beauty spots and places of interest on Exmoor until 1937, when Blue Motors acquired the rights to operate the excursions. Bryant Brothers sold their two sun-saloon coaches separately, these being advertised as: 'Two 1930 sunshine Chevrolet 14-seater coaches, certificate to end 1937 and 1938. Mechanically perfect, bargain at £45 each.' The firm continued as furniture removers, using two Ford lorries for this work.

A very lively operator was Eli Ford of the Premier Garage, Alcombe. He was in business by 1922 as a charabanc proprietor, running excursion trips from Minehead and Dunster. Following the sale of Hardy Central Garage to the National company he decided to try his luck on two motor bus routes from Minehead. Accordingly, his yellow and light-blue painted Mascot Safety Cars appeared on the Porlock Weir route, where they competed with Blue Motors, and that to Dunster village, where the competition was principally with National. Typical 'pirate' tactics were adopted: waiting in Porlock until a few minutes before the competitor was due, then running just in front, picking up the waiting passengers. Further services were started to Luccombe and Roadwater, both at one time served by Hardy's but subsequently abandoned. Eli Ford's fleet numbered six buses and coaches by 1933 when, in order to get rid of their troublesome competitor, Western National bought out the Mascot services, leaving Eli Ford to dispose of his AJS, Chevrolet and Reo vehicles separately.

Out on Exmoor in February 1920, a Mr Heberden of Exford began running a Model T Ford van, converted to carry fourteen passengers. With this he maintained a regular return service for passengers and goods, four times a week

A Mascot Safety Cars A.J.S. bus with the owner and his staff outside the garage at Alcombe. (CD)

Eli Ford, proprietor of Mascot Safety Cars, Minehead, stands beside YA2954, a fourteen-seater Unic which he bought in 1922. (AM)

Porlock Weir, with the harbour and the Anchor Inn, was a much favoured destination from Minehead. Motor buses on the regular daily services and chara-bancs on excursion trips can be seen turning in the distance. (AM)

(more often in the busy season) between Exford, Winsford, Bridgetown and Dulverton railway station, 'also calling twice weekly for Withypool'. On Mondays, Tuesdays and Wednesdays he left Exford at 9.30am, returning from the station at 2.30pm, but on Fridays there were two round trips, departing Exford at 7.30am and 4pm. The return fare between Exford and Dulverton was five shillings and sixpence. This little vehicle covered 8000 miles a year over the rough moorland roads but in January 1927 was succeeded by a fourteen-seater Overland owned by Commander Q.B. Preston-Thomas, RN, of Fixcombe. Using the title 'Exe Valley Carrier' the former naval officer ran between Exford and Dulverton twice weekly, and through to Exeter once a month. In 1930 he was bought out by the Great Western Railway, who thereafter classified the service as 'cartage' (goods only) and stopped carrying passengers.

From Dulverton two services of station motor buses, one of them connected with the Lion Hotel, the other with the Lamb, met all trains. The hotels competed fiercely for passengers, offering inducements such as first-class hunting, with hunters and hacks available for those wishing to ride, as well as free fishing and billiards. Open or closed motor cars were on hire. The buses

"My granddaddy liked his possum stew, so whenever he caught one, he'd cut off the tail for me to play with."

It was her grandmother who noticed how much she liked music: "She traded one of her milk cows for a neighbour's piano, and I taught myself to play listening to the church accompanist." Bobbie composed her first song when she was seven, My Dog Sergeant Is A Good Dog, which was later resurrected as a fun part of her act. Her Mississippi roots would be the in-

the rockabilly sing... olds. By 1967 she had attracted the attention of Capitol, and one of her songs, Mississippi Delta, was to be her first single with them. On the flip side was Ode To Billy Joe. We know what happened after that.

Of course it's a teenage death song, with Billy Joe, who was clearly close to the girl narrator, committing suicide off the Tallahatchie Bridge for reasons unknown. The key phrase is when the girl's mother tells her: "That

minutes long, and vital clues were cut out of it. Bobbie never would answer the question of what was thrown and why Billy Joe committed suicide, and would insist that the real theme of the song was the narrator's family's indifference to the tragedy.

Theories about what went over the bridge range from a baby to an engagement ring to a knife which the girl wrested from Billy Joe's hands after he had threatened to

commit suicide... a pop lyric we are discuss... it doesn't do to get too... bearing in mind the... phobic family ties... throughout the song, it... believe that the girl c... had a child, or even an... without somebody in t... cottoning on.

In 1976 a movie purpo... swer the question, but... didn't. It made Billy Jo...

It's hot on board

BABY boomers

MUSIC AND MEMORIES OF A NEW GENERATION

LAST week I was in a coach in which the air conditioning broke down - and Sod's Law being alive and well in 2005, it was on one of the half-dozen days in the year when air conditioning wouldn't have been a bad idea.

The problem is, you can't open windows any more. The coach is air-conditioned, you see.

So we sat and sweltered and glared at posers in open-topped sports cars and looked back on the days of civilisation when you felt too hot on a bus and simply slid the top pane open.

Then again, perhaps it wasn't as civilised as all that, or simple. Some of the most bitter rows I ever saw my parents involved in were over the last half-inch to which a draughty skylight might be opened, or in later years, over the volume at which the wireless was acceptable.

Bobbie's bridge lyric still a mystery

With Terry Manners away, **JOHN HUDSON** takes a look at the life and times of Sixties Mississippi singer-songwriter Bobbie Gentry

Talent: Singer-songwriter Bobbie Gentry, who taught herself to

LAST week in this column Terry Manners was telling us the story of Carole King, one of the great women singer-songwriters of the Sixties. That got me thinking about another.

Bobbie Gentry was not nearly as prolific as Carole, but her Ode To Billy Joe, a number 13 hit here in 1967, is still one of the most talked-about songs of the decade.

Roberta Lee Streeter was born in Chickasaw County, Mississippi, in 1944. Her parents divorced when she was very young, and she spent her early childhood living with her grandparents on their dirt-poor farm outside Woodland in Chickasaw's Mississippi Delta country. "We didn't have electricity, and I didn't have many playthings," she once said.

Traded a cow for a piano

spiration for many of the songs she wrote.

In her early teens she moved to California to live with her mother, and taught herself to play guitar, banjo, bass and vibes.

At 14, after seeing the film Ruby Gentry, in which Jennifer Jones played a Southern belle "who wrecked a whole town, man by man, sin by sin", she decided she liked the sound of "Bobbie Gentry", and used it when she began performing in a local country club while still at high school.

The tale is that she was heard and encouraged there by Bob Hope and Hoagy Carmichael, which is the subtle difference between being a kid in Palm Springs and almost anywhere else in the world.

Things moved on, and around 1964 she recorded two duets with

nice young preacher Brother Taylor dropped by today, said he'd be pleased to have dinner on Sunday, oh, by the way, He said he saw a girl that looked a lot like you up on Choctaw Ridge, and she and Billy Joe was throwing somethin' off the Tallahatchie Bridge." The identity of that "something" has been the subject of hot debate ever since.

Part of the mystery lies in the fact that after her brief chart career, Bobbie Gentry has genuinely managed to disappear from public view.

She presumably has pots of money, and there are rumours that she is still in music production, but always shy of publicity, she has succeeded in shunning it more than most.

ONE theory is that her

Dulverton station is situated a mile and a half away from the town at Brushford. Pictured here in 1952, this Bedford bus (AAF66) of Greenslade's Garage, Dulverton, met all trains and conveyed passengers and their luggage. It was the successor to the horse-drawn omnibuses which plied on the route. (ABC)

met every train at the station and carried not only guests for their respective hotels but any member of the general public wishing to ride. In addition Charlie Hoskins, a former driver of the Lion bus, had permission to stand his car at the station.

With two buses and a taxi competing for limited traffic things could get heated. One day in 1922 Daniel Roberts, the driver of the Lion bus, then owned by Mr F.W. Dullingham, went to meet a train with orders to pick up a lady who had made a prior arrangement to travel in his vehicle. Charlie Hoskins arrived in the forecourt before Daniel Roberts and put the lady in his vehicle. On arrival Daniel heard the passenger say she wanted to go to Mrs Harvey's and he realised that Charlie had taken his fare. 'That's my lady,' he said 'I've been sent for her.' This provoked an argument, during which Charlie Hoskins punched Daniel Roberts in the face. Both men duly appeared in court and Charlie was fined £2 with £2.2s. costs.

Heat of a different kind was generated in 1926. One August evening Bert Bryce, the driver of the Lamb bus, was returning from the station when his vehicle caught fire. The petrol tank immediately became a raging furnace, but Bert acted with great presence of mind. He drove the bus to the side of the road, stopped it and with the two passengers jumped into the road. There was no chance of saving anything and the bus was burnt out, only the metal chassis and, curiously enough, the rubber tyres remaining. For some days afterwards the remains lay in a hedge hollow and were an object of interest to passers-by.

The Dulverton town and station service continued until 1956, although in later years only one operator, F. Greenslade and Son, maintained it.

In the late 1920s and early 1930s Messrs Spencer and Anderson of the Carnarvon Arms Garage, adjacent to Dulverton station, had a fourteen-seater Fiat charabanc available for hire. By 1934 this facility was being provided by Mr J.H. Mainerd. He was certainly a man of many parts, his shop in Dulverton High Street being a fishing-tackle depot with salmon and trout licences issued and artificial flies a speciality: 'Dressed to any pattern at the shortest notice'. James Henry Mainerd was also a toy and fancy goods dealer and umbrella repairer. Then he started a motor-coach enterprise. His Chevrolet, Bedford and Dodge vehicles took pupils to school at Bampton daily and carried local people to the fairs and carnivals at Bridgwater, Barnstaple and Bampton, as well as on trips to the Exeter pantomime, fare four shillings and sixpence. He eventually sold the coach business to Batten and Thorne of Tiverton in 1945.

In Dunster, the Ell family of Staggs Head House had long been active in the life of the community. Mr Samuel Ell, apothecary and dispenser at the Cottage Hospital, was famous for his home-made marmalade, advertised as

Three motor cars owned by Spencer and Anderson of the Carnarvon Arms Garage, next to Dulverton station. On the left is a Gladiator driven by Mr Anderson; the others are Napiers. (PA)

'Wholesome and delicious, guaranteed to be the purest on the market – as supplied to the House of Lords'. This was available in glass jars at 6d., 9d. or 1s. ('Ask your Grocer for it'). For anyone troubled by corns, Ell's 'Korncure' (price ninepence halfpenny) was claimed to cure hard or soft corns and was available not only in Dunster but also at Timberscombe, Porlock and Luxborough. Samuel Ell was also clerk to the Parish Council and the Burial Board and deputy registrar of births, deaths and marriages . His wife, Edith Mary Ell, was a dress-maker. Their son, Clifford John Ell, served in the Navy and returned to Dunster to build a garage in St George's Road, the bricks for which arrived at Dunster station and were then hauled up to the village.

By 1925 Cliffie (as he was known) was running a Maxwell charabanc, conveying holidaymakers staying at Dunster beach on tours over Exmoor. During the 1930s he operated a Bedford all-weather coach and three taxis and, in addition to summer excursions, his programme included journeys to the meets of the Stag Hounds during the season. His main competitor was Tom Heard of Timberscombe, who was also licensed to run tours from Dunster. Ell's coach operation ceased in 1940 due to wartime restrictions, the coach being acquired by the Burnell family of Wootton Courtenay. In the post-war years Cliffie took the village cricket and football teams to away matches on Saturdays, using a large old Buick. This car was known as 'Old Tick Tick' because of its wooden wheels, which made a noticeable clicking noise as they gradually dried out and the spokes loosened. When this became too bad the wheels were removed and replaced by the spare set, which had been kept 'swelled up' in a barrel of water until needed. Ell's services stopped when Cliffie died in the 1950s.

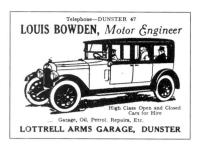

Dunster High Street in the 1920s with a noticeable absence of traffic: just a horse and cart, a few cars and an open charabanc. (PC)

Louis Bowden's garage at Dunster Steep in the 1950s with a gathering of motor cyclists on a London to Land's End trial. Early motorists obtained petrol from chemists' and selected stores in 2-gallon cans until, in 1920, the A.A. hit on the idea of providing a limited number of roadside pumps for their members. The idea caught on and soon filling stations could be found everywhere. (KA)

Mr W. Burnell of Wootton Courtenay started in business in 1919 when he came out of the Army. Passengers were first carried to and from Minehead in the early 1920s, when they rode in a sidecar attached to his motor cycle. He later bought a Maxwell car, then launched out into motor buses, running weekly market services from Kings Brompton to Taunton and to Minehead. These ceased in the 1930s, leaving only a link between Wootton Courtenay and Minehead. For a time Bill Burnell was in partnership with Geoff Pugsley of Wheddon Cross but in the early 1930s the business was split, Bill continuing with the garage and buses, Geoff taking the cattle haulage side. As well as taking villagers to town for shopping and entertainment, Burnell's bus picked up visitors in Minehead at 3pm during the holiday season. It took them to Venniford and Wootton Courtenay for a walk, followed by tea at the Dunkery Beacon Hotel or one of the two tea gardens before catching the tastefully liveried beige and mid-brown bus back into town. During the Second World War the local Home Guard were carried and over the years from the 1930s onwards generations of local schoolchildren travelled daily on a Burnell's bus.

The first bus ever from Wootton Courtenay had been operated by Mr Bill Prescott of Luccombe in the early 1920s. His first vehicle was a Daimler which could be adapted for use either as a lorry or, fitted with seats, to carry passengers. Later he used a purpose-built Fiat.

Men like these built up services that depended entirely upon a local need

Wootton Courtenay in the 1930s with Burnell's fleet of buses outside their garage. DV1675 is a 1929 Chevrolet; AYA677 and AAF66 are Bedfords, new in 1934. (EPA)

and they started the process of breaking down the sheer isolation that was the lot of so many who lived in remote habitations on and around Exmoor. As an instrument of social change the country bus probably had no equal.

Motor transport played another increasingly important role. In the late 1920s the National Omnibus and Transport Company began a regular express coach service between London, Minehead, Lynton and Ilfracombe, running at weekends during the summer holiday season. It catered for an growing number of travellers for whom the long journey was an opportunity to see the beauties of the countryside from the comfort of a luxurious all-weather motor coach. The return fare between Lynton and the capital city was £2 and all seats were reserved in advance.

Until October 1928 the speed limit for coaches had been twelve miles an hour but then an increase to 20 mph gave the impetus for expansion. By 1934, when the limit was raised to 30 mph, regular long-distance express coach services were well established and fares had been reduced to highly competitive levels. A return journey between Minehead and London cost only £1.10s., between Lynton and London £1.14s. 9d., and a system of connections made it possible to travel by coach to or from virtually any settlement of any size in the country at a price generally well below rail fares. Although the coach which left London at 9am did not arrive in Minehead until after 6pm and reached Lynton some two hours later, the express motor coach had became a formidable competitor to the railways in long-distance passenger transport. At Minehead and Lynton, Royal Blue Express Coaches, owned by Western and Southern National, were a familiar sight for many years until they became part of the National Express network of today.

Together with Scarlet Pimpernel and Blue Motors, the major operator in the Minehead area was the Western National company. In the early 1920s the National Omnibus and Transport Company was seeking opportunities to inaugurate motor bus services in many parts of the South of England. They expanded into the Westcountry and commenced operations from Taunton in 1921, but their services did not reach Minehead until 1927, when the business of Hardy Central Garage was acquired. National took over bus routes linking Minehead with Dunster, Exford, Dulverton, Taunton and Bridgwater and they also inherited Hardy's excursion business. However, a shortage of vehicles in 1928 led to the abandonment of the Exford route. Here they were replaced by Tom Heard of the Lion Hotel, Timberscombe, who used the name of one of the old Minehead and Lynmouth coaches, the Red Deer.

Tom's maroon-coloured buses with a stag's head emblem on the sides brought Exford, Withypool, Winsford and Timberscombe people into Minehead for shopping and on two evenings a week a special bus catered for those attending performances at the Queens Hall, Minehead. The Red Deer service was also popular with summer visitors who travelled out to start walks over Dunkery or to visit Tarr Steps. For those wishing to see the countryside from the comfort of the bus, a circular tour left Minehead each afternoon for Wheddon Cross, continuing under Dunkery to Exford, where there was time for tea. The return was over Winsford Hill to Winsford village, then along the main road from Dulverton, through Wheddon Cross.

In 1929 the road motor services of the Great Western Railway were merged with those of National into a new company, the Western National Omnibus Company Ltd. They gradually bought out most motor bus competitors in and around Exmoor. Apart from Eli Ford and the Blue Motors, already mentioned, Western National's acquisitions included the Imperial Service of H.V.G. Williams from Watchet, the Lavender Blue service of Thomas Motors to and from Taunton, Dunn's Motors service, also from Taunton, and Tom Heard's Red Deer service between Exford and Minehead, as well as his tours from locations including Minehead and Dunster – all these in the 1930s.

Burnell's bus service to and from Wootton Courtenay was withdrawn in 1959, because the conductress was going to have a baby. She was Mrs Joan Burnell, the daughter-in-law of the proprietor and, because she had to give up her job, it was felt that the income from running the service did not warrant employing anyone from outside the family. The Burnell family continued to run school buses and hire out coaches and Western National provided a replacement bus service for Wootton Courtenay village.

The summer of 1932 and a walker, wearing sports jacket, shorts and knee-length stockings, waterproof slung over his shoulder, makes enquiries from the driver of a Morris bus of Dunn's, Taunton. Behind is a Devon General Leyland on the through service from Exeter. (OS)

Western National vehicles pass along The Avenue, Minehead, in procession en route to Lynmouth. During the summer months the arrival of a train at Minehead station brought an influx of passengers for the bus connection to Lynmouth. The heavily laden coaches had an unmistakeable whine as they climbed Porlock Hill in low gear. (AM)

In the post-war years Western National virtually monopolised bus services in the area but for excursion passengers they faced stiff competition from the high-quality vehicles and service provided by Scarlet Pimpernel and Blue Motors, the three firms now being the sole providers of excursions from the area. A far cry from the colourful and highly competitive days of the 1920s and 1930s.

Today, with greater freedom to travel, brought about by the private car and improved road conditions, it is difficult to imagine the heyday of coach touring. Between the First World War and the 1960s as many as 44 coaches left Minehead daily, carrying up to 1400 passengers to all the places of interest and beauty in the locality. The town's claim to be 'the gateway to Exmoor' was well justified.

Motor Servics from Lynton and Lynmouth

The first motor charabancs to enter Lynton and Lynmouth in the years before the Great War came from other parts of the country and it was not until the summer of 1914 that the first locally based vehicle took to the roads. Its owner was Mr W.G. Attree, to whom it was acknowledged 'the thousands of people

Lynmouth with a large touring car and an open charabanc ready for excursions. This area changed dramatically as a result of the Lynmouth flood disaster of 1952. (PC)

who every year enjoyed the scenery of the Watersmeet valley owed a debt of gratitude'. He founded Myrtleberry at the beginning of the twentieth century, developing the area upstream from the Lyn Rock spring as far as Watersmeet. An attractive walk was formed, with a graceful light bridge leading to the Myrtleberry Refreshment House, with lawns on which were placed deckchairs and tables.

The Attree family were also involved in a Temperance hotel in Queen Street, Lynton, with electric light and heating, home-produced food from their own poultry farm and garden produce. Their business interests also included the sale of mineral water, obtained from a spring on the East Lyn River, near Myrtleberry, and marketed as 'an invigorating tonic'.

Mr Attree had a rather unusual taste in 'pets', keeping two or three large monkeys of a rather uncertain temperament at his house. Unfortunately, one of the animals escaped and made its way into Lynmouth, where it alarmed several people with its antics. The animal even entered some of the houses and one can only imagine the consternation that its sudden appearance in a doorway must have aroused! It was pursued and Mr Charley Pitt tried unsuccessfully to lassoo it, but efforts to recapture were to no avail and its owner, knowing its dangerous character if provoked, soon appeared with a rifle and shot the ape.

Mr Attree did not earn universal praise when, after purchasing a Daimler 35-horsepower charabanc, he proposed to run a public service between Lynmouth and Watersmeet. A petition against the plan was 'numerously signed' and presented to the Council, from whom Mr Attree had sought permission to run.

The local authority were in a quandary. There was a strong body of opinion firmly against the use of motors on the valley road. The objectors felt that there were already problems of traffic congestion, the road was narrow and over-crowded and the motor would frighten the horses, be dangerous to walkers and a general nuisance. Others felt that progress was inevitable. If permission were refused now, they would have to agree later.

However, when Mr Tom Jones asked on what grounds a licence could be refused or restricted, it transpired that this was possible only if the bye-laws would be contravened. These had been drawn up in 1884, 30 years previously, and there was nothing about motors in them. Accordingly the Council was judged to have no powers to prevent a motor service and the application was approved.

A debate then arose about the possibility of widening the Watersmeet road and this was given added impetus when Mr Attree applied for a second licence, for an eight-seater. In an effort to allay fears about safety, some elected members were given a trip in the motor and, when it came to a decision, some people hinted that 'those gentlemen on the Council to whom Mr Attree had given a free ride should support it'. Approval was given.

It appears that the motors plied between Lynmouth and Watersmeet, competing with various horse-drawn vehicles, until at least 1916. They may have stopped then because of the wartime fuel shortage. The Daimler remained in Mr Attree's ownership until May 1919, when it was sold to Elliott's Garage of Lynton for further service as a lorry. In the post-war years Mr Attree did not resume operation and in 1926 he retired from Myrtleberry to live at Ilfracombe. When he died, two years later, his funeral service was held at Countisbury, but few at Lynton and Lynmouth knew of it until afterwards. On hearing of his death many paid tribute to the achievements of Mr William Gregory Attree.

His pioneering of motor coaches led others to follow, the first of whom was John Ward Holman of the Valley of Rocks Hotel. In June 1916 he placed in service a green-painted, 25-horsepower Guy capable of carrying fourteen passengers. This, together with two Studebaker landaulettes, was used to convey visitors on excursions around the district, offering an alternative to the traditional horse-drawn carriage.

In the operation of the motor charabanc John Holman was associated with Alfred Oxenham of Priors Cottages, Lynmouth. The Oxenhams were an old Lynmouth family and Alfred had traded as a jobmaster, hiring out horse-drawn carriages, since before the turn of the century. He was also a coal retailer. His brother Arthur's family kept the Ye Olde Cottage tearooms. The exact nature of the arrangements between Messrs Oxenham and Homan is unclear but in the post-war years Alfred Oxenham ran a fourteen-seater Model T Ford charabanc and a Fiat hire car on excursions from Lynmouth and later, when he added a Chevrolet coach and three large touring cars, started a regular service during the summer months between Lynmouth and Watersmeet.

Jack Fry was one of the drivers and one quiet afternoon, outside the garage, he picked up the tours board and asked Mr Oxenham if he should 'paint him'. A passing holidaymaker, thinking he was being addressed and not quite understanding the Devon dialect, replied: 'No, thanks. I went to Paignton yesterday.' In 1922 the ownership of the Valley of Rocks Hotel passed to Messrs Shiers and Pond and at some stage the original Guy passed into Mr Oxenham's sole ownership.

During the 1920s other motor operators started up in the twin resorts. Marmaduke Clapp took the name of the cottages in which he lived as the title for his tourers and the Lynn Cliff Cars ran daily excursions in summer to all places of interest on Exmoor, as well as to Ilfracombe and Clovelly. He was a member of the Urban District Council and in 1929 'Brother Clapp' performed songs and recitations at a public 'smoker' in the National Schoolroom held in connection with the Lynton branch of the Church of England Men's Society. The vicar 'kindly provided liberally for smokes and gave a short address'.

Clarence Wakeham was another who saw that a living could be earned by taking visitors on motor trips. During the 1920s he was in partnership with Sydney Willshere, a local fruiterer and greengrocer who at the time of the Lynmouth flood disaster was the stricken town's sole remaining contact with the outside world. His premises were flanked by buildings and escaped much of the force, so he gave what amounted to a running commentary on events to those at the top of the hill. Clarence Wakeham became the sole proprietor of the Blue Cars and ran a frequent regular service in summer, linking Lynmouth and Watersmeet, although this was a hard road to work and the season was short. About three times a day his 'Doone Valley Coach' continued on through the narrow but charming road to Brendon and Malmsmead, where a break was allowed before the bus returned by way of Countisbury Hill to Lynmouth.

While travelling through Brendon, Wakeham's bus passed the Stag Hunters Inn. This establishment was in the hands of Joseph Totterdell and was famous among a large clientele of hunting and fishing people, students, writers and

A 1932 Bedford used after the Second World war by Clarence Wakeham of Lynmouth, who ran a regular summer service to and from Watersmeet. Three times a day the bus continued on through Brendon to Malmsmead (for the Doone Valley), returning by way of Countisbury.(RO)

BLUE MOTORS

C. Wakeham, Proprietor.

TELEPHONE : LYNTON 97

TIME TABLE
of the
DOONE VALLEY
and
WATERSMEET
SERVICES.

Station Work.   Cars for Hire.

DOONE VALLEY SERVICE

Daily from Aug. 1st to Sept. 17th, 1934

Outward Journey.	WEEKDAYS a.m.	a.m.	p.m.	p.m.	p.m.	SUNDAYS p.m.
Lynmouth dep. *bottom Cliff Rly.*	10.30	n Sat. 11.30	2.30	n Sat. 3.15	5.15	2.45
Watersmeet ,,	10.40	11.40	2.40	3.25	5.25	2.55
Hillsford Bridges ,,	10.45	11.45	2.45	3.30	5.30	3.0
Rockford ,,	10.55	11.55	2.55	3.40	5.40	3.10
Brendon ,,	11.0	12.0	3.0	3.45	5.45	3.15
Malmsmead arr. *for Doone Valley*	11.15	12.15	3.15	4.0	6.0	3.30

Return Journey.	WEEKDAYS a.m.	p.m.	p.m.	p.m.	p.m.	SUNDAYS p.m.
Malmsmead dep.	11.30	n Sat. 12.30	4.30	n Sat. 5.0	6.5	n Sat. 6.20 / 5.45
Oare Church ,,	11.35	12.35	4.35	5.5	6.15	5.50
County Gate ,,	11.40	12.45	4.45	5.15	6.25	6.0
Brendon Post ,,	11.50	12.55	4.55	5.25	6.35	6.10
Countisbury ,,	11.55	1.0	5.0	5.30	6.40	6.15
Lynmouth arr.	12.10	1.10	5.10	5.40	6.50 / 7.5	6.30

Brendon Return Passengers must meet Coach at Brendon Post for Lynmouth.

Special late Afternoon Journey (Reverse Route)

Lynmouth dep. ...	n Sat. 5.45	*Special Notices.*	
Countisbury ,, ...	6.0	n Sat.—**NOT SATURDAYS.**	
Brendon Post ,, ...	6.5	Tickets are available on day	
County Gate ,, ...	6.10	of issue for any Blue Motor	
Oare Church ,, ...	6.15	Coach.	
Malmsmead arr. ...	6.20		

Fares.

From		Waters-meet	Hillsford	Rockford	Brendon	Doone Valley
Lynmouth	To	9d.	1/-	1/6.	2/-	2/6
Watersmeet	,,	—	3d.	1/-	1/6	2/-
Hillsford	,,	—	—	6d.	1/-	1/9
Rockford	,,	—	—	—	6d.	1/6
Brendon	,,	—	—	—	—	1/-

From		Oare Church	County Gate	Brendon Post	Countis-bury	Lynmouth
Doone Valley	To	6d.	1/-	1/6	2/-	2/-
Oare Church	,,	—	6d.	1/-	1/6	2/-
County Gate	,,	—	—	6d.	1/-	1/6
Brendon Post	,,	—	—	—	6d.	1/-
Countisbury	,,	—	—	—	—	1/-

Return Fares: From Lynmouth to Doone Valley 3/6, Brendon, 2/6. Watersmeet 1/3   Children under 12 half-fare.

Passengers at Lynton can book at F. I. Berry's, Tobacconist, by the Post Office, Lynton.

LYNMOUTH AND WATERSMEET

Half-Hourly Service from 12.30 to 4.30 p.m.
Hourly Service from 4.30 to 6.30 p.m.
Single Fare 9d.   Return Fare, 1/3

BOOKING OFFICE—
Opposite Bath Hotel, Lynmouth Street.   Phone 97.

---

holiday visitors. It was the scene of great excitement at pony-gathering time, when the animals brought off the moor into the yard. There followed a memorable party and a sale at the inn yard. It was not merely as successful business people that Joseph and his wife were held in high regard; in 1923 the local press reported that Brendon and the surrounding hill country parishes of Countisbury, Culbone and Oare 'seemed to give themselves over completely to holidaymaking' on the occasion of the couple's silver wedding anniversary. Tributes were paid to the integrity and acumen with which they conducted their business and also for the part they had taken in the social and family life of the 'hill country'. The report continued:

In such festive events as harvest home, dancing and whist drives to benefit local charities, the Brendon District Agricultural Society, of which Mr Totterdell is the Hon. Treasurer, and in many other ways, 'mine host and hostess' have given many happy days and nights to a widely scattered moorland district and one of the loneliest in winter time.

Mr Totterdell was a devoted Churchman, a Freemason and, in politics, 'a tower of strength to the conservative cause'. In public life he was a Guardian and District Councillor for Brendon and tried hard to improve the terrible roads of his own and neighbouring parishes. He also ran a small transport business and in the 1920s his Chevrolet coach took guests and others staying in the neighbourhood on trips over Exmoor and occasionally further afield.

Tom Jones had been a dominant force in coaching from Lynton and Lynmouth before the Great War and in the early post-war years he continued to run horse-drawn carriages to the Doone Valley and to the Hunter's Inn (both leaving daily at 11am, fare 7s.6d.). He also inaugurated daily motor charabanc trips to Ilfracombe and to Clovelly and his nephew, Witney Heywood Jones, son of 'Mr Bob', put into service an AEC charabanc. In 1921–2 they both sold their excursions business to Hardy of Minehead but 'Mr Tom' retained the Lorna Doone motor service to and from Minehead. This was managed for him by Ernest Porter, who also oversaw the Hardy operations locally.

An open coach line-up photographed at Lynton church in about 1929. Left to right: Clarence Wakeham's 1921 Fiat (TA771), a National Omnibus Company Guy (UU7724), a Crossley owned by Ernest Porter (FM2172), and a large touring car. (PC)

On a fine day a National Guy charabanc, hood folded back so that the passengers can enjoy the sunshine, waits at Lynton to depart on an excursion. (RG)

On the sale of the Hardy business to the National Omnibus and Transport Company Ltd in 1927 Ernest Porter acquired the excursions from Lynton and Lynmouth and, on the death of Tom Jones in 1928, also took over the Lorna Doone service. These he ran until 1930, when they passed to Western and Southern National, for whom he remained an agent for some years. Hardy's Lynton operations included motor bus services to and from Ilfracombe and Barnstaple, but National found that many of the vehicles acquired from Hardy were in a poor condition and unfit for further service.

With insufficient vehicles available to cover all commitments there was a dramatic cut-back in services, including those which operated to and from Lynton and Lynmouth. This presented an opportunity for Thomas Slann, whose family owned the Glanville boarding house, a creamery and a motor repair garage in Lynmouth. He already ran a taxi and so it was not a major step to purchase a Reo fourteen-seater charabanc, the driver of which was Percy Lavercombe. Percy drove it on summer excursions and on the former Hardy Sunday evening run through Minehead to connect with the main line train at Taunton station.

Several local men had large touring cars available for hire by private parties and these were also used on public excursions, the fares charged being the same as on a charabanc trip. Among the motor car proprietors were C.W. Burgess of the Oakleigh Boarding House at Lynmouth, who used a large maroon Crossley to carry people to and from Watersmeet, competing with the charabanc services of Alfred Oxenham and Clarence Wakeham. Up at Lynton, a retired policeman, Robert Sparks, drove a black Studebaker and was succeeded by Ernest Bentall, owner of a garage in Burville Street. The latter ran a rather splendid Rolls Royce dating from 1925. An appropriate name for the neighbourhood was W.B. Ridd, who favoured an Austin car for his motor excursions over Exmoor and as far afield as Torquay and Glastonbury.

One of the earliest to offer a motor-car hire service in Lynton was Prideaux' Garage. The firm, who originated as coachbuilders in Barnstaple, turned to motors and proudly claimed to be one of the oldest Austin agents in the country as well as being North Devon agents for Morris cars. Cars were hired out with chauffeurs and in 1910 John Prideaux opened a branch in Lee Road, Lynton. Although they did considerable business carrying private parties, they never succeeded in gaining permission to run public trips from the resorts, each time facing strong objections.

During the 1930s Alfred Oxenham sold his coach business to Western National but continued to use Sunbeam, Buick and Morris cars on 'Hackney Car Trips' to the Doone Valley, Clovelly, Cheddar Caves and on an 'Exmoor Circular Tour'. Plenty of time was allowed for sight-seeing and reliable drivers were employed. Terms were based on bus fares with parties of four or more conveyed at reduced prices, much to the chagrin of Western National, who thought, incorrectly, that the sale conditions prevented this. Alfred Oxenham's Guy coach was included in the purchase and it is surprising that the large company chose to continue to use a 1916 vehicle, designs of the 1930s having greatly improved both comfort and reliability. However, the old-timer was described as 'in quite good running order', despite having a very old Bosch magneto and not being fitted with an electric lighting set, relying on oil side and tail lamps.

Hire-car work was greatly reduced after the Second World War as the more well to do, who had formed the bulk of the clientele, brought their own vehicles on holiday. There was still a demand for bus services and coach tours, Clarence Wakeham and Western National resuming their services on the Watersmeet road. The latter and Marmaduke Clapp offered the visitor a programme of coach tours to all places of interest in the district.

In the late 1940s two brothers called Mansell came down to Lynmouth, apparently from Bristol, and took over first Clapp's Lynn Cliff Cars, then Wakeham's Blue Motors. Trading as Mansell's Blue Motors, they used examples of the very popular and reliable Bedford 29-seater coach. The characteristic whine of these petrol-engined vehicles was heard on ten shilling and sixpenny day trips to Clovelly and Westward Ho!, afternoon excursions over Dunkery Beacon (fare 7s.3d.) and five shilling evening tours, leaving at 7.30pm, returning at 10.30pm – all starting from the Glen Lyn Car Park. The regular service from the Cliff Railway at Lynmouth, through Watersmeet and the Doone Valley ran every summer but already loadings were being affected by the greater use of private cars.

Mansell's sold out to Western National in 1955, giving the latter a virtual

A former Scarlet Pimpernel Leyland Cub (YD9811), now with Mansell Brothers, edges between cars as it leaves Lynmouth Esplanade on the Doone Valley bus service on 6 August 1952, shortly before the village was devastated by flood water. (ABC)

A Western National Bedford (HYB264) goes through the water-splash at Malmsmead, a popular stopping point, in June 1953.

monopoly in the area and bringing to an end a long tradition of locally owned transport services.

The former Hardy-Colwill's motor bus route between Lynton and Barnstaple was, from 1929, operated by the Southern National company. For many passengers the road service was more convenient than the picturesque but slow narrow-gauge trains and in 1935 the Southern Railway decided to close the line. Despite protests buses took over, but in order to cope with some unusual features of the route the bus company purchased specially designed vehicles.

In addition to passengers, local people going in and out of town as well as others travelling to or from the trains at Barnstaple Junction station, there were mail bags, churns of milk and many other packages to be conveyed between Lynton, Parracombe, Bratton Fleming and Barnstaple. Buses with large rear goods compartments were used and these were known as the 'Lynton Mailers'. They remained in service until the 1950s, by which time the carriage of goods had considerably reduced.

The mailers covered a route of steep gradients through some wild, open countryside and the weather could be fierce, particularly around Blackmoor Gate. It was essential that every effort was made to get the mail through and in

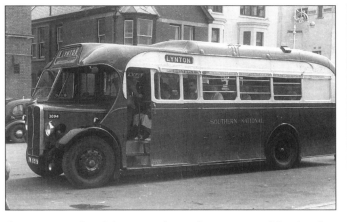

deep snow the drivers and conductors would take the vehicles as far as they could then, if at all possible, carry the mail forward on foot. There are many instances of buses having to be abandoned, the crew and passengers seeking shelter overnight at a nearby farm.

The route was used by holidaymakers from South East England who travelled by train to Barnstaple Junction, then transferred to the bus for the onward journey to Lynton. They would stream off the train in numbers to be met by a mailer and one or two relief buses. Mail and milk churns would be loaded, passengers luggage stowed on the roofs and the buses would set off for Lynton. For many visitors this was their first experience of narrow roads and steep hills and the long haul up through Bratton Fleming would bring exclamations of horror: 'These aren't roads, they're barely lanes! And so steep!'

However, worse was to come when the bus turned off the main road and started the descent into Parracombe village. As it negotiated the narrow lane, then seemingly plunged into an abyss, panic would set in. Newcomers to North Devon were convinced that the brakes would not hold and a horrible death was imminent; they would be dashed against a building at the bottom. One man's terror was expressed through a constant and loud blowing of his nose all the way down.

(Above) A rear view of a Southern National bus used on the Barnstaple–Lynton route. Milk churns and mail bags are ready for loading into the luggage compartment. On one occasion a sweep was going out to Bratton Fleming but was too dirty to ride in the bus. He was put in the mail compartment but forgotten until the bus reached Lynton. (CPC)

(Above left) A 'Lynton Mailer', TK6519, at The Strand, Barnstaple. These AEC vehicles, which had large rear compartments to carry mail, milk churns and other goods, were bought by Southern National after the closure of the Lynton and Barnstaple Railway in 1935 and remained in service until the 1950s. (CS.CPC)

Over half a century after the last horse-drawn coach left Lynmouth for Minehead, passengers board a 1974 Volvo of Venner's Scarlet Coaches for the journey to Minehead. They will enjoy a swift journey in a luxurious vehicle, in marked contrast to the hardships endured by the early travellers. (RG)

Eventually they arrived at Lynton and a nervous band of travellers thankfully dispersed to their hotels and guest-houses. During their stay anyone willing to listen would be regaled with stories of 'our horrendous bus ride from Barnstaple'.

Ilfracombe to Exmoor by Motor

In the years after the Great War the use of motor vehicles increased rapidly and soon the horse-drawn conveyances were a thing of the past. The popular daily trips from Ilfracombe to Lynton and Lynmouth became the sole preserve of the motor charabanc. The use of motors gave the opportunity to venture further afield over Exmoor and the Doone Valley, Dunkery Beacon and Tarr Steps were now regularly visited by parties of visitors from Ilfracombe.

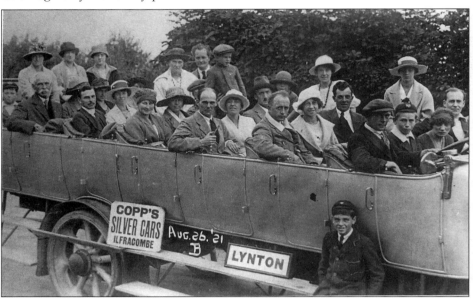

A motor charabanc of Thomas Copp and Sons, Ilfracombe, on an excursion to Lynton. (AM)

A Maudslay charabanc of Copp's Silver Cars, Ilfracombe, climbs out of Parracombe village, conveying a party of visitors on an excursion to Lynton and Lynmouth. (PC)

The Village, Parracombe. 15107.

A motor in Parracombe waits for passengers to return. The wall of the garage on the right carries signs advertising Spencer Moulton Tyres, Mobil oils and B.P. Motor Spirit. (PC)

A 1930s Bedford coach of Lovering Brothers, Combe Martin, on a tour to Lynton stops for a break in the Valley of Rocks. Some of the passengers stay close to the vehicle and admire the view while the more adventurous have clambered up the hills. (RG)

So numerous became the conveyances of all kinds running from Ilfracombe that in summer the visitor had no difficulty in selecting a trip at almost any time of the day. The conveyances were well appointed and in the charge of capable drivers. The return fares varied, but most were reasonable as there was considerable competition.

In 1925 the situation was described thus:

In the last few years motor tours have become very popular at Ilfracombe, affording as they do a comfortable and inexpensive way of viewing the surrounding countryside. Several enterprising firms cater for the public in this way; the motor has greatly added to the convenience of Ilfracombe as a holiday centre.

With over 80 vehicles vying for trade at the peak, competition was inevitably fierce. A contemporary report reads:

> Various complaints have been voiced by visitors of the touting of the motor charabanc booking clerks. Although most of the visitors take the whole thing in a good natured manner, they are given a bad impression of the townsfolk which will ultimately effect a fall in the number of our visiting population.

There were a limited number of tours over Exmoor that could be run, and with so many trying to attract passengers it was essential they were either cheaper, different or better. Cutting prices was the road to ruin, as several found out.

One local proprietor found a different way to drum up trade for his trips to Lynmouth and the Doone Valley. He placed a blackboard outside his office bearing the words:

> 'Then the sound of a shot rang through the Church and those eyes were dimmed with death. Lorna fell across my knees and a drop of blood came down the yellow altar steps. The only sign of life remaining was the drip of bright red blood...' Visit this wonderful spot by booking here for the Doone Valley.

The local press approved, commenting: 'This advertisement attracts considerable attention and seems to gain more trade than by the irritating system of touting.'

Unusual emphasis was laid on some aspects of excursions from Ilfracombe to Exmoor. One tour that circled the moor, taking in most of the beauty spots and some fine moorland scenery, was summed up as 'a grand Exmoor trip which takes one through Simonsbath to South Molton, a quaint borough which few visitors to Ilfracombe would otherwise have the opportunity to visit'.

Making one's tour seem better than the others was another means of promotion. The usual route for a trip to Exmoor and Minehead was by way of Exford and Dunster, returning via Lynmouth and Watersmeet. One operator, trading as The Grey Cars, decided to differentiate his tours from those of his competitors and proclaim himself to be sole operator of the Tarr Steps Tour. Forsaking any undue modesty, he stated in his advertisement:

> No other daily tour in the British Isles offered such an exquisite variety of natural beauty. No explanation can do justice to this magnificent tour. It is Nature's most picturesque tour. To appreciate that such a feast of natural beauty exists you must see it!

His competitors combined to retaliate, issuing a special note to visitors:

> Do not be misled that the Tarr Steps Motor Tour takes in all the Minehead Tour, because IT DOES NOT. Our Minehead Tour is not to be equalled by any other motor drive in England for beauty or variation of scenery. ... Return Fare Ten Shillings.

The Grey Cars took exception to this and put out a notice which began: 'Can an Ordnance Survey Map Mislead You?' It went on:

> Do not be confused by leaflets issued by a few local operators. Any map of Exmoor will convince you that our TARR STEPS TOUR embraces the

whole of the 10/- Exmoor and Minehead Tour, except a very short uninteresting five miles from Exford to Wheddon Cross. To eliminate this
uninteresting portion of the Minehead Tour the 'GREYS' five years ago
added the prettiest portion of Exmoor to the ordinary Minehead Tour, viz
Winsford Hill – Tarr Steps, Dulverton and the Exe Valley, which is not
included in the 10am Minehead Tour. 'THE GREYS' thus make the TARR
STEPS Tour the finest daily trip in the British Isles. This is not our opinion
but the opinion of every passenger who has taken the tour.

It ended with a poem which included the following lines:

If it's the Exmoor Hills you Visitors are seeking,
We'll take you across Dunkery Beacon.
How the 'Combine' are to do this we await with smiles
As their coaches don't go near Dunkery for at least three miles.
No doubt they intend to hire Airplanes or Tanks
or fit wings to their coaches to fly over the banks.
'THE GREYS' ask all Visitors to study a map.

After the Second Word War the daily exodus from Ilfracombe to Exmoor
continued but the number of operators steadily reduced as the private motor
car brought more and more of the holidaymakers to the area. Instead of numerous coaches of various shapes, sizes and colours manoeuvring along the narrow
moorland roads and lanes, streams of cars with city drivers, terrified of the
unaccustomed narrowness, steepness and constant twists in the road, struggled
to reach the beauty spots such as Watersmeet, Malmsmead, Dunkery Beacon,
Tarr Steps, Dunster and Horner Woods.

Order out of Chaos

We have seen how the explosion in the number of public service vehicle operators after the First World War led to fiercely competitive practices which,
inevitably, eventually resulted in calls for tougher controls. Until the early 1930s
responsibility for licensing motor buses, charabancs and services rested with
local authorities, of whom Minehead Urban District Council was one. They
relied upon the Town Police Clauses Act of 1847 for their powers but this had
been drafted before the invention of the internal-combustion engine and its
deficiencies, together with the inconsistent way in which the powers were

*With more than 80 charabancs
competing for excursion traffic
from Ilfracombe, proprietors had
to work hard to attract custom.
Copp's Silver Cars and Gubb's
Lucky Violet Cars used touts,
painted signs, chalkboards,
photographs and tear-off leaflets
to grab the attention of passers-
by. (RG)*

LICENCE No. **H** 75509

BADGE No. **H H** 18663

THE WESTERN TRAFFIC AREA,
BEACON HOUSE,
QUEEN'S ROAD,
BRISTOL 8.

WESTERN TRAFFIC AREA
THE GAUNT'S HOUSE,
DENMARK STREET,
BRISTOL, 1.

LICENCE TO DRIVE A PUBLIC SERVICE VEHICLE.

ROAD TRAFFIC ACTS, 1930 to 1947.

THIS LICENCE is issued by the LICENSING AUTHORITY for the WESTERN TRAFFIC AREA and authorises—

> John Thomas Newton
> Star Garage
> Down Thomas
> Plymouth

*Strike out the words which follow if not appropriate.

to drive a public service vehicle* of the type or types shown in the schedule below.

This licence shall have effect as from *July 13th 1954* and shall continue in force for three years from that date.

Date of issue *July 13th 1954*

Fee 3/-

Signature of licensee (*see Note 1*).............................
(In ink.)

SCHEDULE.

Type or types of public service vehicles which the licensee is licensed to drive.

SINGLE DECKED.

NOTES.

(1) The licensee must sign this licence in ink in the space provided above immediately on receiving it; but must not write anything else on it.

(2) The licensee must notify the Licensing Authority of any change of address within 7 days of such change.

(3) This licence does not absolve the licensee from the obligation to obtain a licence to drive under Part I of the Act of 1930. The latter licence has a stiff cover in which this licence when folded into six can conveniently be kept.

(4) If this licence covers all types of single deck public service vehicles, the holder may drive heavy goods vehicles without a special licence for that purpose under Section 31 of the Road Traffic Act, 1934.

(5) Any inquiries regarding this licence should be addressed to the Licensing Authority at the address given at the top.

[OVER

exercised, meant that the laws were out of date and of limited use. A truly British solution was invoked: a Royal Commission to sort things out. Their report resulted in the Road Traffic Act of 1930, which was revolutionary and sweeping. Among its provisions were the abolition of the maximum speed limit of 20 miles an hour for cars and motor cycles and the raising of the minimum age for car drivers to seventeen. It also introduced compulsory third party insurance and imposed new controls on buses and coaches.

From 1931 conductors and drivers had to hold a licence, the latter taking a special driving test, before being granted the much prized right to wear a Public Service Vehicle driver's or conductor's badge. Driving hours were limited and all vehicles had to obtain a Certificate of Fitness. No regular service could be run without the consent of newly created Traffic Commissioners and other operators and the railway companies could object to proposed services. The latter frequently availed themselves of this opportunity, seeking to stifle all competition with rail services. Traffic Commissioners had the final word, although the Act did allow an appeal to the Minister of Transport.

Every licence to run a bus service stipulated the exact times, days, routes, stopping places and fares. For excursions and tours the number of coaches to be used on any one tour, or overall on any day, was stated and routes to be followed specified in great detail. Within a short time every coach operator running tours from Minehead was forced to charge standard fares.

Local authorities were also permitted to object to applications and an example of Minehead Urban District Council influencing events occurred in 1938. Hawkins Brothers, proprietors of the Scarlet Pimpernel Coaches, applied to run a regular service from the sea front to North Hill which would have allowed both residents and visitors to reach an area of spectacular landscape.

From the minutes of the Council meeting held on 15 March, it is clear that the members were unimpressed:

The Clerk reported upon the application of Messrs Hawkins Bros. for a proposed bus service between the sea front and the Camp Ground....
Proposed by Councillor Hemingway and seconded by Councillor Johnston and resolved that the Council object to the proposed bus service on the grounds:
(a) The proposed bus service is to be run on a route which is unsuitable for traffic.
(b) That the service will seriously affect the amenities of the district, especially along the route.
(c) That the service is not needed.
(d) That for general reasons the Council are of the opinion that to inaugurate such a service would be a retrograde step.

The account of the meeting in the *West Somerset Free Press* gives a little more detail:

Motor Coaches to Camp Hill
From Notices and Proceedings of the Traffic Commissioners, which the Clerk produced, it appeared that Messrs Hawkins were proposing to apply for permission to run a motor-coach service at frequent intervals daily between the sea-front and Camp Hill, via Martlet Road and St Michael's Road, from 12th May to 30th September.

Mr Hemmingway moved that the application be opposed, pointing out that it was a narrow road up there and, to children living in the cottages on the route, buses would be exceedingly dangerous. Mr Johnston, who seconded, considered it would spoil the rateable value of property on the hill, and Mr Bergin also objected on the ground of danger.

Mr Berry, advising the Council against being too hasty in their decision, said he believed that there were many people wishing to go to the hill who would be very glad of the convenience thus offered. The hill was one of Minehead's beauty spots and if the Council could encourage visitors to get up there without undue risk he thought they should, to some extent, meet them. Mr Sage agreed with Mr Berry. Old people and others who could not easily get on to the hill should be given some form of convenience.

Mr Brandram was another objector. It was not a strong road up there, he stated, and it would be ploughed to pieces. And it was the only way one could walk and take a dog in safety.

The Hawkins brothers withdrew their application, perhaps in order to maintain the goodwill of the authority in the future. The ability of the Council to object

| | | | NEW SERVICES. | | |

STAGE CARRIAGE SERVICES.

H.5898.—**W. and J. Hawkins** (trading as Hawkins Bros.), of The Avenue, Minehead, Somerset, between **Minehead** (Sea Front) and **North Hill** (Camp Ground), via Parade, War Memorial and St. Michael's Church.

(1) To operate the following service from 12th May to 30th September:—

Weekdays.

		a.m.	a.m.	a.m.	p.m.	p.m.		p.m.
Sea Front ..	dep.	9.45	10.45	11.45	12.45	2.0	and	8.0
The Avenue	,,	9.50	10.50	11.50	12.50	2.5	hourly	8.5
St. Michael's	,,	9.57	10.57	11.57	12.57	2.12	until	8.12
North Hill	arr.	10.7	11.7	12.7	1.7	2.22		8.22

		a.m.	a.m.	p.m.	p.m.	p.m.		p.m.
North Hill	dep.	10.15	11.15	12.15	1.15	2.30	and	8.30
St. Michael's	,,	10.25	11.25	12.25	1.25	2.40	hourly	8.40
The Avenue	,,	10.32	11.32	12.32	1.32	2.47	until	8.45
Sea Front ..	arr.	10.37	11.37	12.37	1.37	2.52		8.52

Sundays.

		a.m.	a.m.	p.m.	p.m.	p.m.	p.m.		p.m.	p.m.
Sea Front ..	dep.	10.0	11.0	12.0	1.0	2.15	2.45	and	7.15	8.15
The Avenue	,,	10.5	11.5	12.5	1.5	2.20	2.50	half-	7.20	8.20
St. Michael's	,,	10.12	11.12	12.15	1.15	2.27	2.57	hourly	7.27	8.27
North Hill ..	arr.	10.22	11.22	12.22	1.22	2.37	3.7	until	7.37	8.37

		a.m.	a.m.	p.m.	p.m.	p.m.		p.m.	p.m.	p.m.
North Hill	dep.	10.30	11.30	12.30	2.15	2.45	and	6.45	7.45	8.45
St. Michael's	,,	10.40	11.40	12.40	2.25	2.55	half-	6.55	7.55	8.55
The Avenue	,,	10.47	11.47	12.47	2.32	3.2	hourly	7.2	8.2	9.2
Sea Front ..	arr.	10.52	11.52	12.52	2.37	3.7	until	7.7	8.7	9.7

(2) To charge fares in accordance with the following schedule :—

```
Sea Front.
 —    —    The Avenue.
2d.  4d.  1d.  2d.  St. Michael's.
3d.  6d.  2d.  4d.  1d.  2d.  North Hill.
S.   R.   S.   R.   S.   R.
```

S.—Single fares. R.—Return fares.

To pick up passengers on the forward journey at Sea Front only for points beyond the Parade, and on the return journey not to pick up passengers in the Parade for Sea Front.

had proved to be influential.

Right at the outset of licensing Scarlet Pimpernel had experienced the powers vested in the Traffic Commissioners. The day tour to Lynmouth and the Doone Valley was one of the most popular. To widen its appeal even further the Hawkins brothers wanted to run to a timetable allowing passengers to alight at any point and rejoin a later journey. It seems that they had started such an operation shortly before the introduction of the new legislation in 1931. Their application to continue was firmly rejected in the face of determined opposition from other operators. It was held the objectors had a prior claim and should now be protected. The Scarlet Pimpernel service had to cease and henceforth their passengers had to remain on one vehicle, observing the usual tour route and stops.

The strict controls imposed by the Road Traffic Act of 1930 and successive legislation was to last for over half a century. New problems of monopoly and inability of firms to adapt to new demands then resulted in new legislation which inter alia deregulated the industry and opened up the concept of competition between operators once more.

Part Four
SCARLET PIMPERNEL COACHES

The Early Years

As we have seen, three firms came to dominate public transport in the Minehead area in the years following the Second World War. Providing many of the local and long-distance bus services was the Western National Omnibus Company Ltd, whose history is recorded in *The Years Between*, Vols 1 and 3, by R.J. Crawley and F.D. Simpson. Similarly, the story of Porlock Blue is covered in *The Blue Motors Remembered*, by Roy Lee. However, the story of the third operator, Hawkins Brothers' Scarlet Pimpernel Coaches, has never been published.

The proprietors William (Bill) and Jack Hawkins owned and managed the business for more than three decades. Then, after the company merged with its main rivals, Blue Motors, to form Scarlet and Blue Motor Coaches, the two brothers, as majority shareholders, managed the combined businesses until they retired and the company was wound up in 1966.

The brothers came from a family of six boys and two girls. They were at first brought up in Exeter, where their father, Fred Hawkins, was a coachman. Their grandfather had been a well-known builder in the city. During the early years of the twentieth century the family moved to Brushford, where Fred Hawkins traded as a jobmaster from a property near Dulverton station. Towards the end of the Great War they moved again, this time to Minehead, where Fred established himself as a horse-dealer and hunting and livery stable proprietor. His premises were at the rear of, and formed part of, the renowned coaching hotel, the Plume of Feathers, which dominated the Square at that time. This important landmark, whose elegant façade added distinction to one side of the Square, was later demolished in what can only be described as an act of vandalism, to make way for a row of shops with no particular architectural merit.

Standing outside Allenhayes in Minehead, the highly polished Leyland coach LYC691, new in 1950, waits to set off on one of the most popular afternoon tours, going over Dunkery and then to Horner Woods for tea. (RL)

(Left) Jack Hawkins (MH)
(Right) Bill Hawkins (MH)

Fred Hawkins became an established figure in the hunting and polo-playing society of Exmoor, the Plume of Feathers stables being the base for visiting horses, including those of the Indian princes who played polo on Dunster Castle Lawns.

With a family tradition of coaching, it is not surprising that the brothers Bill and Jack Hawkins decided to make their careers in transport following their return from active service in the First World War. Although the family were keen on horses, they saw that the future lay with motor traction and so, during the summer of 1920, they purchased a Hupmobile touring car (registration number Y8273) and a Wolseley cabriolet (Y8947). These were used as taxis, plying for hire on the sea front, near the Bungalow Café. Shortly afterwards they bought a Rolls Royce adapted for use as a motor charabanc and this signalled the start of the Scarlet Pimpernel Coaches. Over the decade there was steady expansion and by 1930 five of the latest type of all-weather coaches were in service.

The choice of the Scarlet Pimpernel name came about as a result of the Great War. The Hawkins brothers were called up for military service and, being an

Fred Hawkins, father of Jack and Bill, astride one of his hunters in the yard of the Plume of Feathers, Minehead. (MH)

The cobbled yard of the Feathers, accessed from Holloway Street, was a substantial complex bordered by garages and stables. Fred Hawkins and his family ran the livery stables and lived on the first floor of the buildings on the left. In the early days of Scarlet Pimpernel the coaches shared the area with the horse-letting business. (KA)

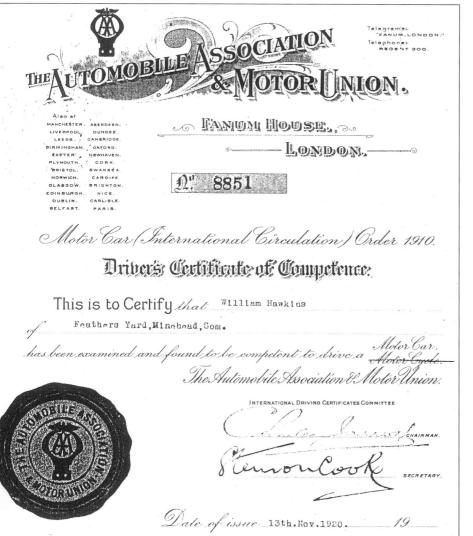

Driver's Certificate of Competence issued to Bill Hawkins in 1920, when he was 22 years old and presumably had a contract which necessitated driving on the continent. In accordance with the Motor Car (International Circulation) Order, 1910, motor cars taken abroad had to be certified as 'suitable for use on the highways of a foreign country' and the driver had to be examined and found competent. The Royal Automobile Club, Automobile Association and the Motoring Union were authorised to issue certificates of competence, the need for which was dispensed with in 1926, when the International Driving Permit was introduced.

expert horseman, as were all his brothers and sisters, Bill found himself in the Hussars. However, he soon transferred to the Royal Flying Corps, where he became an Observer in No. 100 Squadron. He flew in what now seems to be a very vulnerable machine, the FE2B, but at the time it was regarded as being a very successful bomber.

The dangers faced by early aviators were soon all too apparent as in April 1917 Bill was shot down, captured and sent to a prisoner-of-war camp in Germany. The living conditions and food in the camp were very poor, and the prospect of a lengthy stay did not appeal to the nineteen-year-old. At the third attempt he succeeded in escaping and was later decorated with the Military Medal for his exploits.

It has been suggested that it was his penchant for escaping and the association with the fictional hero of the novel by Baroness Orczy, *The Scarlet Pimpernel*, that gave rise to the name used by the Hawkins brothers for their charabancs. The reality is different but equally romantic. It appears that the wild flower of that name was the only flower that flourished in the prison camp. Out of this grew an affection that led to the scarlet pimpernel being enshrined in the name of the company that became Bill's life's work. Although the choice of fleet name was partly a subjective one, it proved to be a shrewd business move, as the scarlet livery of the coaches commanded attention wherever they went.

Management and Drivers

Starting any new business venture calls for courage, commitment and above all, hard work. This was certainly true for those starting in the coach trade in the highly competitive market that existed in Minehead immediately after the First World War. The challenge was compounded by the problem facing any business which relies upon the summer holiday trade: obtaining sufficient income during the season to see it through the long, lean winter months.

Unlike some of their main competitors, the Hawkins brothers did not have the luxury of acting as a board of directors, with staff to oversee the running of the business. Every managerial and operational task required their personal attention, so stamina and capacity for hard work were an essential ingredient of the success achieved throughout their working lives. For them it was a seven-day-a-week operation from spring until autumn and even in winter there was much to be done.

Scarlet Pimpernel charabanc at Cheddar Caves around 1923, a sixteen-seater Fiat driven by Bill Hawkins. Open-top travel was part of the fun and a spare wheel and fire extinguisher were essential equipment. (MH)

During the season the working day started early. There were the booking offices to open, coaches and drivers to be allocated to the various trips. Then passengers to be loaded and morning departures supervised. The main surge of activity came around midday as preparations were made for the highly popular afternoon tours. From 6pm onwards the coaches would return and in between arrivals motors would depart on the short evening drives. Eventually the last vehicle would return, to be cleaned and prepared for the following day. In between times there was, of course, the serious business of booking passengers for future tours.

No matter how carefully vehicles are maintained, there are often problems. These range from tyre damage to mechanical failures, scratches gained in negotiating the narrow lanes to torn upholstery. This inevitably meant having to work late into the night to ensure that the coach would be ready for service again next morning. Sometimes replacement parts would have to be collected, often from distant suppliers, and this was a task that inevitably fell to one of the partners.

When the season was over and winter came there was still much to be done. In addition to the routine overhaul of vehicles there was a steady stream of work, principally shopping and theatre excursions, as well as private party bookings such as sports teams travelling to away fixtures. Most of these journeys were at what would now be called unsocial hours but they were then seen as just another business opportunity.

If the business depended upon the skill, hard work and enterprise of the two Hawkins brothers, the role of the drivers was also crucial. Scarlet Pimpernel could boast the most up-to-date vehicles kept in immaculate condition. It could claim a tours programme second to none. All this counted for nothing if the drivers were not up to standard. They not only took the passengers to and from their destinations safely but also saw to it that the entire trip was an enjoyable and memorable experience. A good coach driver was a combination of skilled operator, friendly and diplomatic courier and knowledgeable guide. He took great pride in his vehicle and his company.

In 1952 Scarlet Pimpernel, in common with other local coach proprietors, responded to urgent calls for help at the time of an unparalleled local tragedy. On the night of 15 August, following torrential rain, a terrible force of water

Friday, 15 August 1952 will always be remembered in Lynmouth. In one terrible night at the height of the summer season a huge torrent of water cascaded down on to the village, changing it for ever. Homes and belongings were swept away and 34 people were killed or listed as missing. (PC)

rushed down the valleys off Exmoor into Lynmouth, causing devastation and loss of life. In the aftermath Western National, Blue Motors and Scarlet Pimpernel coaches and staff worked tirelessly, helping to evacuate hundreds of people from the stricken communities. No charge was made by the companies for the use of the vehicles and many of the staff gave their services free. It was a terrible time and no one who witnessed the scenes will ever forget them.

Hawkins Brothers employed a core of regular drivers throughout the year. The remainder were seasonal staff but many returned year after year and were familiar figures to those who regularly took their holidays in the town. Scarlet Pimpernel drivers wore a peaked cap fitted with a white cover and a full-length white dust-coat with cuffs and collar in scarlet. On their lapel they proudly wore a red and white Public Service Vehicle Driver's licence badge, the mark of the professional.

Donald Jones, who drove for Scarlet and Blue in the 1950s, recalls being taken on by Bill Hawkins and taught to drive a coach by Bill and the foreman, Charlie Babb. It was Bill who decided when he was competent enough to take the Public Service Vehicle Driver's test. Donald recalls that his working hours were Monday to Saturday, 8.00am–7.30pm; Sunday, 1.00pm–7.30pm.

Although the official starting time was 8 o'clock, if the coach had not been washed and swept out before leaving work the previous evening it had to be done before 7.30 the next morning. No overtime was paid. These may now seem wholly unacceptable conditions but they were taken for granted in those days and numerous drivers stayed with the firm for many years. Transport was in their blood and the comparatively quiet winter months offered some compensation and allowed them to see more of their families.

In his first season Donald worked from July to December, then was taken on again in the following spring on a permanent basis. He remembers that when not required for driving duties, he manned the booking office or stood beside his parked coach talking to holidaymakers and encouraging them to book excursions.

Another driver, Dick Dibble, worked for Scarlet and Blue in the 1950s. He drove an Albion coach which he recalls with affection. The only fault was the petrol system, which was situated close to the engine block and had a tendency to dry up when the heat evaporated the fuel. He remembers how all the drivers took pride in the appearance of their coaches and on the Weston-super-Mare trip, where there was a five-hour stay in the resort, they would polish the exterior panels using Simonize, a famous car wax that is still popular today. To achieve

Driver Dick Dibble stands proudly beside LYC462, an Albion Victor with Duple body seating 29. Dick not only polished the panels but also blackened the tyres to achieve the standard of presentation for which Scarlet Pimpernel was renowned. The head- and side-lights seem inadequate by today's standards. (RD)

the very high standard of finish required a lot of elbow grease was needed.

Dick recalls that many tours returned through the Exe Valley and that up to a dozen coaches in different liveries would return at much the same time. Such a convoy was a colourful sight. Another recollection is that during the winter at least two coaches each year were completely stripped down. All the seats were taken out, everything was cleaned and overhauled and the bodywork resprayed. None of this work was contracted out; the partners and drivers would undertake it all.

The wages in those days were five pounds ten shillings a week but a very good driver frequently more than doubled his weekly wage with tips, or 'nubbins' as they were termed.

Another account of the life of a driver in the late 1950s comes from an unusual source. A young man called Peter Anderson from Dulverton had just completed his National Service, during which he had learned to drive heavy vehicles. He was studying at Cambridge University before going on to a successful career in Occupational Health and Safety that took him all over the world. Peter persuaded the Hawkins brothers to employ him during four summer seasons. The much respected former Blue Motors foreman, Charlie Babb, gave him a trial run and then arranged for him to take the P.S.V. test which he passed first time. So began an experience which Peter describes as one of his most cherished memories.

From Peter we gain an insight of a driver's life. Learning the routes was, of course, essential for a new driver and this knowledge could only be obtained from those more experienced. Peter learned directly from Bill and Jack Hawkins, Charlie Hawkins and Fred Hooper.

Daily orders would be obtained from the main office in The Avenue, adjoining the hospital. Peter remembers this as well run by Bessie Hawkins, a sister of the Hawkins brothers. It took considerable skill to ensure the right size and type of vehicle was allocated for the route and to cover the number of passengers booked on each tour, that the work was allocated fairly among the drivers and their respective knowledge and experience was taken into account.

Many of the routes were a considerable challenge and visiting car drivers were unused to narrow roads and steep gradients. Reversing was a skill they had not entirely mastered. When faced with a large oncoming coach some were inclined to freeze, others to panic and it was frequently the coach driver who had to manoeuvre his large vehicle to allow progress to be made. Thus a high degree of driving skill was called for.

High on the list of priorities for the driver an ability 'to tell the tale'. Stories, facts and general information were gleaned from many sources, some being passed from driver to driver. Peter remembers one story passed to him for the Dunkery tour. He was advised that this should preferably be delivered in a broad Exmoor accent. After passing through Dunster on route for Cutcombe Hill, he should stop close to Grabbist and explain that these were the mountains where the Reverend Alexander (and other variable nominees!) had written the hymn 'All Things Bright and Beautiful'. This went down extremely well with religious passengers but he was never able to corroborate in any way that there was the slightest truth in the story.

Despite the long hours and seven-day working week, all the former drivers recalled their time with Scarlet Pimpernel and Scarlet and Blue with fondness. Perhaps it has something to do with the high degree of personal responsibility and independence they had once they were behind the wheel. The passengers were really 'in their hands' then. It is also likely that there was a sense of pride in working for a successful company, held in high esteem for the quality of vehicles and the service offered.

It is appropriate, therefore, to quote Peter Anderson, one of those drivers on whom the success of the company depended, who told us: 'I shall never forget the pleasure and privilege of driving for Scarlet and Blue and it is still one of my most enjoyable experiences'.

The Tours

Very few seaside resorts can compete with Minehead as a centre from which to explore such attractive countryside. Motor coach tours offered the visitor easy and comfortable access to magnificent scenery and picturesque places, made all the more interesting by the commentary from the driver.

The Scarlet Pimpernel day tours would start at various times between 9am and 10am, depending on the distance to be travelled. This allowed visitors to have a leisurely breakfast before making their way to the pick-up point. Afternoon drives generally left at 2.30pm and all tours returned between 6.30pm and 6.50pm, in time for the evening meal at the boarding houses and hotels. Then, after dinner, short evening drives were available and, at a fare of two shillings or half a crown (2s.6d.), these were very popular.

Mr Richard Ford recalls that in his boyhood before the Second World War his family would take their annual fortnight's holiday with his paternal grandparents at Luxborough. They managed occasional trips to Minehead and these were achieved by walking to Dunster where, at the Forester's Hotel, they would catch either a National bus or that of Tommy Heard, who ran the Red Deer coaches and was also licensee of the Lion at Timberscombe. They could then book for an evening drive on the Scarlet Pimpernel. Riding in an open charabanc with the hood folded back on a fine summer's evening he recalls as a pleasurable experience. The tour would go from Minehead, through Dunster, Washford, Roadwater, Luxborough (where they would alight at his grandparents') and then back to Dunster and Minehead. 'It was good value for two shillings,' he remarks.

The Luxborough tour was remembered for another reason by Mrs P. Gillard, who rode on this tour in the late 1920s and early 1930s. She recalls that there were two cottages along the way in which lived rather large families. When it was time for the charabancs to pass the children were all called in, dressed in rags, and made to stand by the roadside with bare feet and wave. The

'Horner Woods for tea' was one of the highlights of the popular afternoon tour over Dunkery. The coaches parked on the nearby green while the drivers enjoyed a cream tea in return for encouraging their passengers to do likewise. This photograph shows the tea gardens in Horner, near Minehead, which are still in use and little changed. (MS)

passengers threw pennies out to them, and they did very well out of it! Mrs Gillard and her cousin tried it one evening but they weren't so lucky.

Mrs Frances Edbrooke is another who remembers the old days, when she went on Scarlet Pimpernel trips. She has happy memories of trips to Webbers Post, then up over Dunkery, returning through Exford. Bill and Jack Hawkins were both very good to stop the coach to point out all the places of interest and, as she says, 'We always felt safe with them.'

There were few restrictions on where tours could travel in what is now the National Park, nor were there the properly designed, strategically located car parks at the most popular localities as there are today. For example, at Tarr Steps the coaches parked next to the Clapper Bridge, while at Horner they stopped on the small triangle between the cottages and the river. At Malmsmead the vehicles parked in front of the farm. It required considerable skill and patience to manoeuvre coaches in and out of parking areas such as these, bearing in mind that coaches from many companies would arrive and depart at about the same time.

The most popular tours were those which travelled across Exmoor to destinations such as the Doone Valley and Tarr Steps. Perhaps the greatest favourite of all went over Dunkery and then to Horner Woods for tea. Prices were reasonable and many holidaymakers regarded one or two trips as an essential part of the holiday. In the 1950s two people could go on the Dunkery Beacon and Horner Woods tour for nine shillings (45p), or to the Doone Valley and Lynmouth for fifteen shillings (75p).

We can get a picture of a typical trip from a firsthand account by Peter Anderson:

It was my third year (1958) driving for Scarlet and Blue when down from Cambridge University on long vacation. For this summer season I had been allocated my favourite coach by far – an AEC Regal with a magnificent 7.7 litre six-cylinder diesel engine and fine bodywork built by Harringtons incorporating a 'dorsal fin'.

I lived at Dulverton at this time and always enjoyed the journeys to and from Minehead in my agile little Austin Mini (a complete contrast in

The village of Horner was popular with holidaymakers and a regular stop on Exmoor excursions. Some visitors rode on the local bus service and here the Western National bus can just be seen at the top of the lane. (PC)

driving characteristics to the mighty Scarlet and Blue coaches!). On this particular day in August the weather was faultless with not a cloud in the sky, making the prospect of any Exmoor tour particularly enjoyable to contemplate.

I arrived (punctually as always!) at the big Nissen hut garage at Mart Road, Minehead, at 8.45am. This garage was capable of housing up to nine of the company's coaches and on this day two were already out on the tarmac in front of the garage, gleaming in the summer sun.

Good morning greetings were exchanged with each of the drivers, all of whom were helpful and friendly to me as a young undergraduate several years their junior. Those present on this occasion were, I think, Fred Hooper, Arthur Willis, Jack Kelland, Trevor Perkins and two of the proprietors' brothers, Charlie and Fred Hawkins. All had given me much past assistance in how to 'tell the tale' to passengers, in order to genuinely please the latter; but also to increase the amount of one's 'nubbins', or tips, at the end of the tour.

I looked at the blackboard on the garage wall. On this was permanently printed a list of tours undertaken by Scarlet and Blue with a space beside each in which the name of the driver undertaking the particular tour would be chalked. Out of all the tours my favourite by far was Lynmouth and the Doone Valley. Why? Firstly, by world standards the

Photographed in July 1955, this 1949 AEC Regal (KYD151) is the vehicle Peter Anderson drove and remembers with great affection. Its well-built Harrington body included a dorsal fin. Happily, the coach has been preserved by a private owner. (RL)

route was (and is) exceptionally beautiful. Secondly, it was the most challenging to drive. Thirdly, the lunch and entertainment down at Lynmouth were always exceptionally good. Fourthly, the cream tea at Cloud Farm, with its Doone Valley setting, was in the same category; and lastly the tour enthralled the passengers more than any other.

Which tour would I be allocated on this cloudless summer day? I approached my AEC Regal satisfied in the knowledge that I had polished her from stem to stern the previous afternoon. As was expected of us, the interior of the coach had also received my attention, had been throughly vacuum-cleaned and was spotless. In short, the AEC did indeed look 'regal' that day!

Climbing into the driver's cab I noted once again the simplicity of the controls and instrumentation: a long vertical gear lever to the left which came readily to hand, a huge handbrake lever to the right, a plain but workmanlike instrument panel which included a speedometer and (vitally) an air pressure gauge to confirm the adequacy of supply to the air brakes! In a somewhat less ergonomic fashion, however, the electrical switches and starter motor button were located downwards and to the right behind the driver. All in all, though, the driving position behind the big steering wheel was superb and the steering (although low geared) was very accurate. Finally the half-cab driving position made it particularly easy to judge the width of the coach by looking across the engine cover to one's left.

The mighty diesel started as always at a touch of the button and I reversed the coach gently on to the hard standing outside the garage. Next I busied myself with checking the oil and water levels and also the tyres and tyre pressures (very important with the inner tyres on the back axle, as low pressure in these was not readily discernible when standing alongside the coach). These duties complete, I washed my hands and donned the stylish white and scarlet driver's jacket which we were expected to wear and which undoubtedly added to the professional image always conveyed.

The phone rang. Fred Hooper answered and started chalking drivers' names against the tours listed on the blackboard. Jack Hawkins had assigned the other drivers to the full day tours, Ilfracombe, Buckfast Abbey, Wells and Cheddar. Would I be truly lucky on a summer day such as this and get my favourite tour, Lynmouth and the Doone Valley? To my great joy Fred chalked up that I had indeed been assigned to that tour. I was asked to bring the AEC round to the main office and advised that I had 28 passengers that day, 24 of whom I would pick up in The Avenue, and four by the church in Porlock.

I drove the coach gingerly through some of Minehead's traffic-crowded streets (yes, even in those days this was often the case). There assembling on the pavement outside the booking office were my passengers. Somehow, in those days, all the passengers were inherently respectable and always appreciative of the service being rendered to them. They were a mix of elderly and young couples and always well-behaved family groups.

Jack Hawkins gave me the list bearing the names and seats allocated to each passenger. This was a vital document, used later to ensure that no one was left behind at any of the stops en route. I greeted each passenger personally as they boarded, made sure they were comfortably seated, then jumped up into the cab. With a cheery wave from Jack Hawkins we were on our way.

The response of the big engine was as good as ever, and needed to be with what was coming later in the tour: Porlock Hill with its dramatic bends and 1 in 4 gradients, Countisbury Hill with its similar gradient and other equally steep hills. The four-speed gearbox sang its usual refined song as I

The Regal Cinema and Ballroom during construction in 1934. The hospital can be seen in the background; next to it, on the left, was the principal office of Scarlet Pimpernel. For many years coaches regularly loaded and unloaded on the road frontage outside the office. (KA)

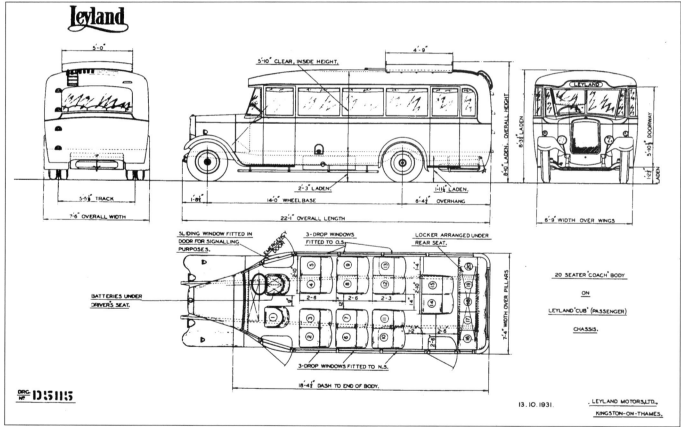

drove, the sound in third gear being somehow always the most impressive.

Out of Minehead we went on the A39 towards Porlock, with North Hill and Selworthy Beacon shimmering in the summer sun to our right and the purple slopes of Dunkery Beacon looking equally beautiful to the left. Down we came to Allerford, where I was briefly able to indicate to the passengers the little gem of a packhorse bridge and beside it the ford in the River Aller from which the hamlet derives its name.

Arriving in Porlock, I noted with relief that waiting on the pavement beside the church were my four additional passengers, one young and one old couple, each person full of smiles at our punctual arrival. As I started off again I reflected that the traffic through the village that day was heavy, the prospect of inexperienced drivers making a hash of their gear changes while climbing the hill a distinct possibility. As Jack Hawkins always said, the key to Porlock Hill was to get into first gear well before the first bend, allow a good distance between you and any vehicle in front, and take the coach on at a comfortable rate.

As I approached the first hairpin bend I had indeed taken that advice and the AEC was all set for the climb. However, the driver of an old blue Morris Ten some way ahead of me clearly had not. I had seen the car approach the formidable corner at considerable speed, evidently in too high a gear. Now as I came steadily round the bend I saw that the car had ground to a halt, and worse still, was rolling slowly back towards me, the brakes obviously unable hold the car on the 1 in 4 gradient.

Only as a last resort could I stop a loaded coach on a gradient such as that and I had already slowed down to a crawl just acceptable to the AEC's patient engine. Coming down the hill towards me, fortunately still some distance away, was a white Bedford Dormobile. I can still see it to this day! I took an instant decision to switch on the headlights as a warning to the oncoming driver that I needed to pull round the stricken Morris and on to the wrong side of the road. A quick fumble with the switches behind me and the headlights were on. The driver of the Dormobile immediately saw my plight, stopped dead and signalled me to come on up the hill, albeit on his side of the road!

I pushed the accelerator hard down on to the floor and to its great credit the engine picked up at once, taking us from a struggling crawl to a steady climb. As I pulled over to the wrong side of the road the old Morris rolled backwards, fortunately missing the nearside of the coach, and lodged itself in the bank. I signalled my heartfelt thanks to the driver of the Bedford Dormobile, noting at the same time some clapping in the coach behind me – directed, I believe, at me rather than the driver of the Morris!

Then on we went up round the next and even more severe bend to the straighter part of the hill, bound for Whitstones at the top. As we climbed I glanced in the rear-view mirror and noticed with a sense of admiration the completely clean exhaust gases being emitted from the side exhaust pipe of the coach were carving a steady furrow in the long uncut grass bank on the other side of the road, such was the amount of power I was having to apply to the climb. That admiration remains with me to this day and was born of two things: the engineering masterpiece which was the AEC and the standard of vehicle maintenance by Jack Hawkins and staff. Only a diesel engine in perfect condition and tuned well could perform under such a load without visible exhaust fumes.

As we continued the climb I signalled to the passengers to look back over the sunlit majesty of Porlock Vale and to the right over the Bristol Channel, which appeared uncharacteristically blue, rather than grey, on this cloudless summer day. A vast expanse of the south coast of Wales was also visible, adding to a panorama which only the north coast of Devon and Somerset can produce.

Our next stop was at County Gate, where Devon meets Somerset. A halt of about half an hour enabled the passengers to visit the little shop and avail themselves of the public conveniences – a most vital factor with the older passengers. Above all, however, I advised them to go to the side of the car park furthest from the road. From there, and only from there, could they see the precipitous drop and fabulous view down into the wooded valley of the East Lyn River. This unexpected vista never ceased to impress the passengers and I always pointed out that they would later be visiting Watersmeet, where the river running far below was joined by Farley Water in an incomparably beautiful setting.

This compact advertising board dating from around 1950 was fixed to the front of the Burgess Café in Porlock. Any tour could be booked up to an hour before departure. No trip listed cost more than ten shillings. (MH/AM)

With all the passengers now comfortable – and apparently still confident in me after my handling of the Porlock Hill incident – we set off again down the A39 en route for Lynmouth and lunch. Calm and careful driving was required for the long descent into Lynmouth via Countisbury Hill, with its 1 in 4 gradient. The safety rule was engage first gear before commencing the descent, stay in this gear right to the bottom no matter how irate a few motorists behind you might become at this slow downward progress.

On the way down I noted the escape lane for runaway vehicles, tyre marks in the sand clearly indicating it had been used recently. The reassuring hiss from the air brakes of the AEC gave me confidence, however, that today at any rate I would not need it. Having safely descended and crossed the relatively new bridge over the East Lynn River I swung the coach sharply left down into the car and coach park. Here as usual I was greeted and directed to my parking position by an attendant who was much liked and respected by all the coach drivers. His name was Fred and quite simply he was one of the world's best, a charming and much decorated old soldier who thought well of his fellow beings and whose good nature was both self-evident and catching.

The time was now 11.45am and my next task was to tell the passengers about Lynmouth, including the flood disaster that had befallen it back in 1952. As usual they listened solemn-faced as I recounted how the original of the bridge we had just come over had been swept away; how the East and West Lyn Rivers had become raging, rock-bearing torrents; how some of the buildings, including the hotel opposite, had been seriously damaged; and, worst of all, how a number of people both in

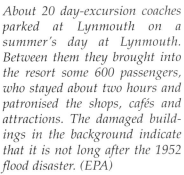

About 20 day-excursion coaches parked at Lynmouth on a summer's day at Lynmouth. Between them they brought into the resort some 600 passengers, who stayed about two hours and patronised the shops, cafés and attractions. The damaged buildings in the background indicate that it is not long after the 1952 flood disaster. (EPA)

Lynmouth and at Barbrook, further up the valley, had lost their lives.

On then to more cheerful things as I explained that the best place to have lunch in Lynmouth was undoubtedly the Cleave Café in the main street, although there were, of course, other choices. (It was not lost on them, I'm sure, that we drivers got splendid free lunches at this pleasant establishment in return for this recommendation.) Next I told them the location of the shops in Lynton and Lynmouth and about the lovely walks to be had at both places. This inevitably led to a brief technical description of the unique water-powered cliff railway connecting Lynton and Lynmouth and the dramatic views to be had when ascending or descending. I had in fact mastered what I thought to be a pretty good description of how this railway worked, but when I tried it out on one of my fellow coach drivers (Arthur Willis I think it was), he said, 'Peter, don't tell 'em all thic technical stuff, they won't understand. Just tell 'em one carriage fills up with water up the top while t'other lets it out down the bottom and up and down 'er goes!'

I always finished my address to the passengers at Lynmouth by telling them about the 18-hole putting course beside the East Lyn River and advising them that as long as they were back at the coach by 2.30pm sharp they might have time for a round. Certainly it was the custom and practice for us coach drivers, having dined freely and nobly at the Cleave Café, to have a putting competition at this lovely location. That day five of us enjoyed a close-run game in which I think I came second only to a true golfer called Norman, who drove for Western National.

Exhilarated at being runner-up, I returned to the coach at 2.15pm to await the return of my 28 passengers. It was always the custom in those days to leave the coach door open in case anyone wanted a place to sit. Sure enough, two old ladies had already returned. They said that they had made it up to Lynton on the cliff railway but had returned for a rest and, characteristically, 'to be sure we don't miss the coach'.

By 2.25pm all the passengers had returned and were eagerly awaiting their next destination, Watersmeet. Waving goodbye to Fred, the jovial coach-park attendant, I drove up the not so steep but decidedly narrow and winding road which was still the A39 but not really entitled to more than B-road status. This was another challenging road on which to drive safely and smoothly, demanding very precise positioning of the coach to allow room for oncoming drivers while avoiding contact with the stone walls on the left-hand side of the road. Of all the coaches I have driven along this route, the AEC, although bigger and heavier than some of the others, was still the easiest and most driveable of them all on this section.

On arrival at the Watersmeet parking ground I saw that two other coaches, one of them driven by the golfer Norman of Western National, had already arrived and I pulled in beside them. The next duty was to point out to the passengers the wonder of the place below them in the valley where, as I had earlier told them, the East Lyn River and Farley Water cascade together. Advice was also necessary that the walk down and back was best suited to the able-bodied and that it might not be wise to partake of a cream tea at the little Watersmeet Café since the ultimate in cream teas was shortly to follow, if they wanted it, at Cloud Farm, near Malmsmead.

As usual two or three of the older passengers demurred a little when they saw the steep access to and from Watersmeet; but also as usual they had only to see the mysterious beauty of the place below them to decide that a visit was nevertheless essential. I always accompanied my passengers down to and back from Watersmeet, not only to help the aged ones but also because I was, and still am, captivated by the place.

By 3.45pm we had all puffed and panted our way back to the coach amid comments such as 'We never knew places as beautiful as this existed

Seen passing through the ford at Malmsmead while on a Lynmouth tour (a route that would not be countenanced for coaches today) is Scarlet Pimpernel Leyland Cub BYC675. It carried a 25-seat Duple body, was purchased in 1936 and gave fourteen years' service. (PC)

anywhere in North Devon.' I now took the AEC on up to Hillsford Bridge and from there on to the most difficult part of the route. Narrow lanes, often with gradients of 1 in 4, leading down to Rockford, through Brendon and on to Malmsmead, where runs Badgworthy Water and the start of what was referred to in those days as the 'Doone Valley'. In fact R.D. Blackmore's great tale of Lorna Doone is pure fiction; there never was a true Doone Valley and the Ordnance Survey maps now more appropriately refer to the upper Badgworthy Water area as 'Doone Country'.

The little bridge over the water at Malmsmead was not wide enough for large vehicles and so to proceed on to Cloud Farm it was necessary to drive through the ford beside the bridge. This presented the opportunity to have a little well-practised fun with the passengers, namely to halt the coach in the middle of the ford, switch off the engine and announce that this was where they got out for the cream tea. As usual a couple of passengers got up from their seats in the apparent belief they had to paddle and I was as quick as ever in explaining that I was joking. Restarting the engine I pulled forward out of the water.

In those days the turn into the little track leading up to Cloud Farm from the Malmsmead to Oare lane was very sharp and narrow for a long coach. It has since been widened. On this occasion, however, through previous practice, I completed the turn in one and we made our way beside Badgworthy Water up to the farm.

Before they dismounted I told the passengers a little about the author R.D. Blackmore and asked whether anyone had read *Lorna Doone*. The response was the normal one: none actually had, yet most had heard of her, knew of the infamous Carver Doone and appeared to believe that these had been real-life Exmoor characters. Some drivers bent on 'maximum nubbins' were wont to imply the story was entirely true, but I always advised passengers that, although brilliantly imaginative, it was indeed fiction. Next I said that anyone who was replete from their lunch in Lynmouth, and who did not therefore want a cream tea, would have time to walk up to the R.D. Blackmore memorial stone in its beautiful setting a little further up Badgworthy Water. They must however be back at 5pm sharp so that we could go on to our final stop for the day at Oare Church.

When they returned to the coach my increasingly suntanned party were as content a group as I can ever remember and those who had managed the cream tea were full of praise for both its quality and for the hospitality of those who had provided it. I now manoeuvred down the narrowest lane of all to Oare Church and was thankful that on this occasion there was not a single oncoming motorist to obstruct our way (and vice versa). At Oare I parked on the gentle slope opposite Oare Manor and told the passengers they had a quarter of an hour to inspect the idyllic little church where, according to R.D. Blackmore, the murderous Carver Doone had shot Lorna Doone during her marriage to John Ridd. I added that they should also look for the missing pane of glass in one of the windows of the church through which Carver had performed this dastardly deed!

Now it was time for our return to Porlock and Minehead and we went from Oare back up to the A39, avoiding at all costs the more direct route via Robbers Bridge over which no large vehicle could pass; there was no practicable ford across Weir Water, either. As we got to the top of Porlock Hill again no words from me could have enhanced the view the passengers had that evening. The late sun was now coming from behind us, creating subtle shadow effects across the Vale of Porlock and giving a golden illumination to Selworthy Beacon and, below it, Selworthy church. In the far distance the Quantock Hills were similarly lit, while to our right Dunkery Beacon was partially in shadow. I engaged first gear and descended the hill in an unhurried fashion, allowing the passengers to drink in the views as we came down to Porlock.

Back at the church I said goodbye to the old and the young couples I had picked up earlier. They said they had never enjoyed a better day tour and stuffed my palm with 'nubbins'. Exactly the same occurred when at about 6.30pm we arrived back at the office in Minehead, having deposited a couple of the passengers near their hotel en route. I slipped into the office, where Jack Hawkins was typically still at work organising the tours for the next day.

I took the ever faithful AEC back to the Mart Road garage and jumped into my little Austin Mini for the return journey home to Dulverton. As I drove back down the Exe Valley I reflected how lucky I was to have a job such as this, albeit only during the long vacations. I also wondered whether my professional career in the future would ever present me with a day at work quite so satisfying and enjoyable as was this one.

In the post-war years much longer journeys were possible, although this was at a time before motorways existed. Every journey was over roads that would now be regarded as sub-standard. Some idea of the range of destinations can be obtained from an advertisement which appeared in the *West Somerset Free Press* during 1953: 'See the Coronation Decorations in London. Visit the Bath and West Show, fare 11s.6d. Blackpool Illuminations in September. Seven Day Holiday in North Wales.' The last two are examples of a new type of tour that was developed after the war. Those living around Minehead could take a coach holiday in other parts of Britain, Scarlet Pimpernel providing driver and coach and making all the arrangements for meals and accommodation. It was a car-free holiday and appealed to many who had cars but did not wish to drive long distances. Increasingly long-distance journeys became an important source of income, with passengers on excursions and private parties going further afield than ever before.

Local people continued to give loyal support to Hawkins Brothers and an example of this can be seen from an incident in 1954. Scarlet Pimpernel had sought permission to run sightseeing tours to London between October and March. This was vigorously opposed by British Railways, who wanted to ensure that travellers went by rail. The extent to which local people, either as individuals or as representatives of organisations, were willing to stand up and support the local firm's application is astonishing, a clear indication that local residents wished not only to travel but to choose with whom they did so.

(Left) An array of boards advertise a wide choice of tours outside the former Blue Motors office in The Avenue, Minehead. A Bedford coach is available for inspection and Dick Dibble is on hand to encourage passers-by to book a seat in the office at the rear. (RD)

(Right) Charabanc stand on Minehead sea front. On the left is a Scarlet Pimpernel Bedford and its white-coated driver; on the right, a Chrevrolet belonging to George Cann. (SW)

Booking Offices and Garages

With over 40 vehicles competing for the custom of those planning an excursion from Minehead, every effort had to be made by motor coach proprietors to get their message over to potential passengers. Because standards of comfort and reliability varied considerably, it was important to let the prospective customer see the type and quality of vehicle in which he or she would travel. Ideally it should be displayed in a prominent place, and what better position could there be than Minehead sea front?

During the 1920s and early 1930s the numerous rival coach operators lined up their vehicles on the sea front immediately opposite what was then called the Bungalow Café and end of the station platform. The coaches lined the road with advertising boards propped up on the pavement or exhibited in the vehicle. The drivers and owners touted for business from passing visitors and those who booked were picked up and set down at this point.

The use of the public highway for this purpose and the nuisance caused by touting were obviously controversial. In the minutes of 1923 the Clerk to the

The Scarlet Pimpernel booking office in The Avenue, Minehead, with the hospital on the right. (SCC)

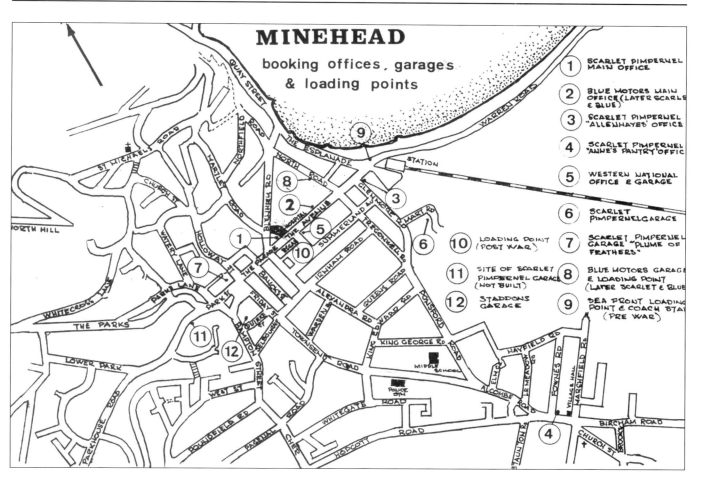

MINEHEAD
booking offices, garages & loading points

1. SCARLET PIMPERNEL MAIN OFFICE
2. BLUE MOTORS MAIN OFFICE (LATER SCARLET & BLUE)
3. SCARLET PIMPERNEL "ALLENHAYES" OFFICE
4. SCARLET PIMPERNEL "ANNE'S PANTRY" OFFICE
5. WESTERN NATIONAL OFFICE & GARAGE
6. SCARLET PIMPERNEL GARAGE
7. SCARLET PIMPERNEL GARAGE "PLUME OF FEATHERS"
8. BLUE MOTORS GARAGE & LOADING POINT (LATER SCARLET & BLUE)
9. SEA FRONT LOADING POINT & COACH STAT (PRE WAR)
10. LOADING POINT (POST WAR)
11. SITE OF SCARLET PIMPERNEL GARAGE (NOT BUILT)
12. STADDONS GARAGE

At the Western National premises in The Avenue a coach tour or a seat on the Royal Blue long-distance express services could be booked, and parcels sent by bus to all parts of the district. On the forecourt passengers queue for buses and an AEC Reliance bus, originally a Royal Blue coach, prepares to depart. (RG)

Urban District Council was instructed to enquire of the Councils of Lynton, Wells, Weston-Super-Mare, Ilfracombe and Torquay as to the arrangements made there for parking charabancs on the highway. However, for about the next ten years there was a lot of talk but no real action and it was the following decade before regulations were brought in to remove the coaches from the sea front.

The operators then moved into The Avenue, loading and unloading outside their respective booking offices. Blue Motors, Western National and Scarlet Pimpernel all had premises in The Avenue, but the latter firm had a serious drawback: they alone had no room to display a vehicle.

No. 39 The Avenue, Minehead, was formerly the main booking office for Blue Motors. This photograph was taken after the amalgamation with Scarlet Pimpernel, during the time when the title 'Scarlet Coaches' was used.

A Western National advertising board used at Minehead to promote the company's services and coach hire facilities. It features a Bristol coach of the 1950s passing Dunster Yarn Market. (SCC)

The Hawkins brothers overcame this by leasing land at the side of the Allenhayes Hotel, at the junction of The Avenue and Glenmore Road. Here there was room to park a coach and it also gave Scarlet Pimpernel two booking offices in The Avenue and 'sandwiched' the opposition. Allenhayes was strategically placed to intercept the substantial number of holidaymakers staying in Alcombe, as it was on their direct road to the sea front. This hotel was owned by the Hobbs family, who had sold their Lorna Doone coach business to the Hawkins.

In an effort to get to as many potential customers as possible, another booking office was opened on the corner of Alcombe Road and Fownes Road. The premises, now a chemist's, were then known as Anne's Pantry. There was room to park one coach. Such was the degree of competition that arrangements were also made with businesses outside Minehead to take bookings and this happened at Dunster Beach and at the Burgess Café, Porlock. The latter was significant as there was considerable local loyalty to Blue Motors, who ran a frequent daily motor bus service to and from Minehead and were well known in Porlock. Bookings were accepted up to an hour before departure time and if the route of the coach tour did not pass through Porlock a car would be sent out specially from Minehead to collect and deliver passengers – service indeed.

From the outset the coaches had been garaged in the Plume of Feathers yard with its substantial covered accommodation and cobbled yard. Somewhat surprisingly, the arrangement whereby Bill and Jack Hawkins' motors shared their father, Fred's, extensive stables of horses worked well. The main disadvantage was the entrance, which came out into Holloway Street through an archway built to take horse-drawn coaches. The motor charabancs had only an inch or so to spare on either side and great skill and some help were needed to make the manoeuvre without damage to the vehicle. As the fleet grew the problem of space for garaging, maintenance and washing became considerable, so some vehicles were dispersed to other garages. Staddon's Garage in Bampton Street was one location used to garage Scarlet Pimpernel coaches.

Immediately following the Second World War, land was purchased at Mart Road and here a rather inelegant but very effective War Department hanger-type building was erected. This housed all the vehicles and had space in the open for cleaning, etc. It is claimed that this building was originally bought for

In the 1930s Hawkins Brothers bought Anne's Pantry, at the corner of Alcombe Road and Fownes Road in Minehead (now a chemist's shop), to use as a Scarlet Pimpernel booking office. The shop continued to trade but a coach stand was constructed in the Fownes Road frontage and is still there. The advertising boards were located behind the low wall and the room with the bay window was the booking office. (MH)

This photograph, taken in the 1950s, shows the narrow arch off Holloway Street, Minehead, leading to the Plume of Feathers yard which early motor coaches had to negotiate. (SW)

This Nissen hut in Mart Road (now the site of a factory shop) was the main garage for Scarlet Pimpernel Coaches immediately after the Second World War, and housed nine coaches and the workshops. The large open area was ideal for washing and cleaning vehicles. Plans for extension of the facilities were never implemented following the amalgamation with Blue Motors. (RL)

This garage in North Road, Minehead (now demolished) was built by Blue Motors in 1935 and passed to Scarlet and Blue after the 1954 merger with Hawkins Brothers' Scarlet Pimpernel. (KA)

use as a village hall at Timberscombe but proved to be too large for that purpose. Another version suggests that it came from Dunster beach and had seen wartime use at a military base located there.

After the amalgamation of Scarlet Pimpernel and Blue Motors in 1954 the use of the latter's splendid purpose-built garage in North Road was available. Earlier the brothers had bought a large plot of land at The Parks, adjoining the former General Post Office, intending to use this for a garage and other facilities. In the event it was never needed and was eventually sold when the brothers retired.

Looking back, it is clear that the Hawkins brothers assembled a substantial portfolio of land and property and this undoubtedly proved to be a sound investment.

The Vehicles

The quality of vehicle operated greatly influenced the chance of success in any motor coach business. The engine power, size and quality of fittings were all important aspects and making the right choice was crucial.

Safety, comfort and reliability were essential factors and no one knew this better than the Hawkins brothers. Over the years they built up a reputation with the travelling public, both for the quality of their coaches as well as for the immaculate condition in which they were kept. Their philosophy was simple: always buy new vehicles with the most reliable engines, fit high-quality coachwork and interiors, keep them clean and presentable. The disposal policy ensured that the fleet was kept up to date, especially in the early days when design was developing rapidly and vehicles soon became out-dated.

Their first charabanc was a Rolls-Royce, and you could not get better quality than that, but it was an adapted car and to continue with the make was not an option. In the early 1920s fast, smooth-running Lancias were favoured. These were fitted with open charabanc bodies with a hood that could be drawn over during inclement weather. These were quite difficult to erect and if there was a heavy passing shower often it would have cleared before the hood was up!

During the 1930s the interior design of motor coaches reached new standards of comfort and finish. This example, used by an Ilfracombe operator on tours over Exmoor, featured patterned moquette seating, curtains at the windows, luggage racks, lighting enclosed in moulded glass and a sunshine roof which could be wound back in fine weather. At Minehead Scarlet Pimpernel also provided a folded rug for each seat for the comfort of passengers in cold weather. (RG)

A wedding party outside Alcombe village hall in a Scarlet Pimpernel 1929 Surrey-Dodge coach. (KA)

Scarlet Pimpernel bought this Leyland Cub 20-seater (YD4771) new in 1932, by which time the open charabanc had given way to enclosed, more luxurious, coaches. Note the two entrances and token running board. A short mast attached to the nearside mudguard helped the driver judge the width of his vehicle. This fine coach was disposed of within four years, which reflects the rate of progress in coach-body design and the need to keep up-to-date. (RM)

When AYC926, a Leyland Lion with bodywork by Beadle of Dartford, was purchased in 1935 its seating capacity of 32 made it the biggest vehicle Scarlet Pimpernel had yet owned. The rearmost seats were raised to improve the forward view, there were curtains at the windows and the canvas roof rolled back. The coach was requisitioned during World War Two but returned in December 1945 and remained in service with the firm until May 1951. (MH)

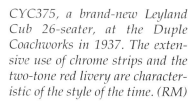

CYC375, a brand-new Leyland Cub 26-seater, at the Duple Coachworks in 1937. The extensive use of chrome strips and the two-tone red livery are characteristic of the style of the time. (RM)

Demand for coaches outstripped supply in the early post-war years and coach firms had to take whatever was available. A variety of vehicles joined the Scarlet Pimpernel fleet, among them 1948 Dennis Lancet KYA572 with bodywork by Thomas Harrington of Hove, one of only two Dennis vehicles run by Hawkins Brothers. (RG)

Closed-in saloon bodies were not popular for touring; they were considered to be stuffy. A motor journey meant feeling the wind in your face.

By the end of the decade there had been a revolution in design and during the 1930s people sought the comfort of the private car in a coach, the word 'charabanc' being dated. Armchair seating of moquette and leather, curtains at the windows, cloth headrests and a streamlined shape to the bodywork were all considered essentials in a modern vehicle. A clock and mirrors were incorporated in the bulkhead; polished wood and chrome fittings and 'jelly mould' light fittings were used to enhance the interior. The open vehicle was not acceptable, although 'all-weather' coaches were quite the vogue. These had a standard saloon with fixed sides, opening windows and a canvas section in the roof that could be rolled back on sunny days.

To cope with the challenging terrain of Exmoor, Bill and Jack Hawkins now generally purchased heavyweight chassis. The products of the Leyland factory in Lancashire were found to suit their conditions well and formed the basis of the business. Backing them up and used on lighter work were Reo, Bedford and Dennis coaches. One of the latter was of a model known as 'the Ace'. The front wheels were set well back behind the bonnet to give a very tight turning circle, but the resultant protruding snout of the bonnet caused it to be known as 'the Flying Pig'.

JYD95, Leyland Tiger with a 33-seat Duple body, was bought new in February 1949 and gave eleven years' service. The substituiton of the initials 'S.P.' for the traditional Scarlet Pimpernel logo was short-lived. (RL)

Hawkins Brothers' only Daimler coach, KYC217, carried a 32-seater body by Beadle of Dartford. Seen here at Horner Green in 1955, in typically immaculate condition, the vehicle gave a smooth ride in the hands of a driver who understood the pre-selector gear change. (RL)

It is noticeable that the vehicles purchased over the years by Scarlet Pimpernel and their great rivals, Blue Motors bore a great similarity. Neither firm was going to let the other have any perceived advantage and they matched each other's every move.

After the Second World War, with demand for new coaches far outstripping supply at a time of scarcity, it was necessary to take whatever was available. Between 1948 and 1950 six different makes of coach entered the fleet and this presented a real challenge for those maintaining the vehicles. The stock of spare parts had to be greatly increased and each make had its own peculiarities and

Still in existence, MYA590 is a 1950 Leyland Comet with 29-seater coachwork by Harrington; the driver sat in the saloon with the passengers. The original livery was two-tone: scarlet on the main body, a contrasting darker red on the front mudguards and around the back wheels.

weaknesses that had to be learned. However, this did not stop the two brothers from maintaining the standards of excellence for which they were renowned.

Considerable care was always taken in applying the Scarlet Pimpernel livery to each vehicle. The dominant colour was an eye-catching scarlet and this was relieved by the careful introduction of sections of darker red, usually in a flash along each side and over the wheel arches. The precise style was varied to ensure that the best use was made of the individual body lines. The company name was discreetly painted in gold letters; it was originally incorporated into a circle, which was later replaced by a diamond. After the Second World War, as the coaches travelled farther afield, 'Minehead' was added after the name.

Off on a day tour to the quaint old fishing village of Clovelly goes MYC801. The combination of a petrol-engined Bedford with Duple 29-seat body resulted in a reliable coach that could negotiate all but the very narrowest lanes of the Westcountry. The curved glass observation panels in the roof gave excellent visibility for the passengers. (ABC)

Seen parked in Summerland Road Car Park, Minehead, in 1954, NYA378 carried a Harrington body on a Commer Avenger chassis. Built in 1951, it gave excellent fuel consumption but it was very noisy and the brakes were hardly adequate for the steep gradients found on Exmoor. No further orders were placed for Commer vehicles. (RL)

During the mid-1930s Minehead blossomed as a family resort. In addition to the other attractions built at the time, such as the Regal complex, this famous swimming pool, said to have cost £20,000, was constructed. Regarded as one of the best of its kind in the country, it was a sad day when it was demolished. (KA)

From time to time changes were tried. For example, a cream flash was incorporated and, on one vehicle, the usual form of name was replaced by a chrome circular monogrammed S.P. However, none of these variations was retained and the traditional livery remained the hallmark of Scarlet Pimpernel until the merger with Blue Motors in 1954.

The 1930s: Scarlet Pimpernel Diversifies

The 1930s were a buoyant time for the resort of Minehead. Public confidence was high, a fact which was to manifest itself with the building of the Regal Cinema and Ballroom and the construction in 1935 of the splendid modern swimming pool on the sea front, now demolished.

On a more mundane note, the Minehead Urban District Council decided in 1935 that the time had come to put an end to the unhygenic arrangement then in place for the collection of refuse. This involved the use of horse-drawn open carts supplied by a Mr Hale.

In September the Surveyor submitted a report upon a demonstration of a Karrier KOLT motor refuse vehicle and a letter stating that the cost of such a vehicle would be £341. A month later the Council considered the matter and their deliberations were reported in the *West Somerset Free Press*.

Mr Judd proposed that the Council at once invite tenders for periods of five and seven years for undertaking the removal and hauling of refuse by means of covered motor refuse carts, these to be similar to that inspected by the Public Health Committee on 18 August and the contractor would be expected to provide the vehicles.

Mr Andrews seconded the motion. Speaking on it, Mr Judd said he had been to the trouble of finding out that Williton Rural District Council, who had such a vehicle, were very pleased with it, and since then had noted that Dulverton District Council had adopted the same line and it was subject to a contract of five years. He had also seen Mr Hale, who was quite willing to purchase the vehicle right away if he should be successful in getting the contract.

The Surveyor was asked if he really thought it preferable to continue the contracting system with motors or whether the Council should purchase two such vehicles and do the collections themselves. He replied that he did not know that it would be a big difference one way or the other. The only thing that led him to rather favour the adoption of Mr Judd's motion was that, assuming the Council had two vehicles, they would have to have a contract with Mr Hale, or somebody else, for certain work that could only be done by horse haulage and to augment the refuse collection on some days when there were double or treble rounds to make. Mr Venn raised the question of whether the proposed vehicles would be able to get on to the tip and deposit their loads where required when the ground was wet. The Surveyor replied that they had this difficulty at present with horse haulage and had to use discretion in tipping where the ground was solid.

Mr Judd affirmed that the adoption of the covered vehicles would meet with the approval of hotel, boarding-house and apartment people, whose visitors complained about the horse carts.

As the Public Health Committee had been trying to improve the system for years and it being felt that the Council should not purchase the lorries until they could house them, Mr Judd's resolution was carried.

Tenders were therefore invited and at the Council meeting on 10 February 1936 the Clerk produced a contract for the hire of refuse vehicles for a period of five years from 1 April 1936. The successful tender was from Messrs Hawkins Brothers, proprietors of the Scarlet Pimpernel Coaches, and it was agreed that

When Hawkins Brothers were awarded the contract to collect domestic refuse in Minehead they bought two Karrier Kolt refuse vehicles similar to this one. With pull-down covers on the body, they were a considerable improvement on the horse-drawn open carts previously employed.

the Seal of the Council be affixed to the contract. The *West Somerset Free Press* gave details of the arrangement. Hawkins Brothers were to receive one pound five shillings for all-day hire. They would be paid eighteen shillings for a morning's work and nine shillings for an afternoon. Saturdays were paid at the rate of eighteen shillings and overtime at three shillings and sixpence per hour.

Minehead now had an up-to-date waste collection service, the rubbish being tipped into the enclosed bodies of the two Karriers purchased by Bill and Jack Hawkins. It was then deposited on the land below the cliffs at Culver Cliff, beyond the harbour, now an open space.

The War and Post-war Years

Since starting in business the Hawkins brothers had built up their business by ensuring they took good care of their passengers and provided a quality product. Their only acquisition of another business had been in 1936, when they took over the Lorna Doone coaches from their good friends the Hobbs family.

By the summer of 1939 they had about eleven coaches and that year seaside resorts enjoyed a record summer. But the clouds of war were gathering and the outbreak of hostilities on 3 September marked not only the end of a period of peace but, as it transpired, the end of an era in social history.

In Minehead, as elsewhere, preparations for war and a likely invasion began at once. Public buildings were protected with sandbags, pill-boxes were constructed along the coast and hundreds of tall posts were driven into the beach at low tide to prevent enemy landings. To everyone's annoyance the pier was dismantled, either to prevent its use in any invasion or because it interfered with the firing of large guns placed on the harbour wall. Just why the enemy should find any advantage in attacking the country via the Bristol Channel was never explained.

In place of the holidaymakers came a flood of evacuees, notably the boys of the Regent Street Polytechnic, who shared the facilities of the Grammar School on a shift system. This arrangement lasted for the duration of hostilities. As the war progressed the town became host to thousands of troops, both British, Canadian and American, who brought with them their tanks. They trained on North Hill, which was placed out of bounds to the civilian population.

There was no place for the luxury coach in this situation, and the impact of war on the business came early, even before the declaration. Bill Hawkins had retained his link with the Royal Air Force as a reservist and in August 1939 was called up for service. It was a serious blow for the family business for 50 per cent of the management to be removed, not to return until the cessation of hostilities in 1945.

Scarlet Pimpernel immediately went into suspended animation. Two coaches, one of them brand new, were requisitioned by the military. Painted in khaki, they were used to transport troops until eventually being returned after the war. The other coaches were 'mothballed' in various locations throughout the town.

Before long a role was found for some of the vehicles: transporting workers, notably to the explosives factory at Puriton, near Bridgwater. Later in the war other coaches, with their civilian drivers, took up permanent contracts to transport troops for the United States army.

The strain on drivers at this time must have been considerable. Not only had all direction signs been removed but their journeys were frequently in the hours of darkness, when they had to cope with blackout conditions. Masked headlights provided only a glimmer of light along roads with no street lighting, cat's eyes or reflective markings.

Surprisingly, in 1942, when the war was at its nadir, a brand-new vehicle entered the Scarlet Pimpernel fleet. This was FYD81, a Bedford with a very utilitarian body incorporating wooden slatted seats. It seems odd that at a time when the supply of new vehicles was so strictly controlled, and so many coaches were unused and in storage, that the purchase of this bus was sanctioned. Whatever the reason, the Bedford performed its wartime duties well but was disposed of immediately after the war.

Eventually the war ended and the coach fleet was refurbished and put back into service. The population, weary of war and deprived for six years of the freedom to travel, took every opportunity to move around. It was long before the ownership of personal transport, so the late 1940s and 1950s proved to be

In an attempt to conserve fuel during the Second World War some buses were converted to run on gas instead of petrol or diesel. The gas was produced by anthracite burners mounted on trailers towed behind the buses. The burners were difficult to light and totally inadequate on hilly roads, and it was a great relief to the bus crews and the engineers when the system was abandoned towards the end of the war. (RG)

(Above left) Bill Hawkins in front of NYD578, a 1952 Bedford with Duple body, a combination popular with many coach operators. The vehicle remained in service until the sale of the business in 1966. (MH)

(Above right) OYA616 was a Bedford SB model with a 31-seat body built by Harrington in 1952; chrome strips were very fashionable at the time. (RG)

(Right) Pictured in Summerland Road, Minehead, in July 1955 is PYB256, a Bedford with 35-seat Duple body, then just two years old. The glass quarter panels in the curve of the roof were phased out: they proved difficult to screen from the sun and gave rise to complaints from passengers. (RL)

boom years for the excursion coach and a highly successful era in the history of Scarlet Pimpernel.

The highly competitive market of the pre-war years gave way to a situation where the demand for travel could hardly be satisfied. Queues formed outside the booking offices of all three Minehead coach operators. At the same time the long-distance coach services were coming into their own, providing travel at highly competitive fares in comparison with the railways. Firms serving Minehead, such as Royal Blue and Associated Motorways, found themselves overstretched at weekends and contracted work out. As Saturday was change-over day for visitors, the Scarlet Pimpernel tours programme on that day was smaller than usual and so the firm's coaches frequently ventured to Bristol, Cheltenham and London, acting as reliefs to the overcrowded express service coaches.

But a threat to the future prosperity of the coach and bus industry was looming on the horizon: the growth in private car ownership.

Scarlet and Blue Unite

In April 1954 the hitherto unthinkable happened: the two main locally owned motor coach businesses in Minehead, the Scarlet Pimpernel of Hawkins Brothers and the Blue Motors of the Porlock Weir, Porlock and Minehead Motor Service Company Ltd, which had been rivals since the 1920s, merged. Not surprisingly, the title Scarlet and Blue Motor Coaches Ltd was adopted.

The exact circumstances which led to the amalgamation are lost in history. However, it is probable that the Board of the Blue Motors, after nearly 40 years of trading, decided the time had come to realise their assets. This is confirmed by the fact that a year previously they had disposed of their highly valued daily

748BYB, a 41-seater Bedford/ Duple purchased by Scarlet and Blue in 1958. The only remaining glass observation panels in the roof are those above the wind-screen; these allowed better forward visibility in hilly country. (RL)

Scarlet and Blue's 498PYB awaits the return of passengers while on a day tour from Minehead. The combination of Bedford chassis and Duple body was adopted as standard after 1954. (RG)

bus service between Minehead and Porlock Weir to the Western National company, with whom they had latterly operated jointly. It must have been a painful decision to sell the route, which was the basis of the Blue Motors business, having been operated since 1916. The company inspired considerable loyalty and affection among the travelling public of the Porlock area.

The key members of the board of Blue Motors would have been lifelong acquaintances of the Hawkins brothers and on the merger two of them became directors of the new company, the formation of which was announced thus:

Scarlet and Blue Motor Coaches Ltd. Capital £56,000.
Directors: William A. Burgess, Edge Hill, Ponsford Road, Minehead
Jack Hawkins, 23 Lower Park, Minehead
William Hawkins, 23 Alcombe Road, Minehead
J. Webber, Holly Cot, The Parks, Minehead
Formed to acquire the businesses of Porlock Weir, Porlock and Minehead Motor Service Company Ltd and Hawkins Brothers, Minehead.

Mr Burgess was a well-known local builder, Mr Webber a partner in a firm of accountants. The Hawkins brothers were majority shareholders and assumed the management of the new company.

Initially it was the intention that the livery of the vehicles would be scarlet and blue in more or less equal proportions. This was not a happy combination aesthetically and was short-lived. Scarlet with a token dash of blue was used but this did not survive long and soon the paintwork was finished in the traditional Scarlet Pimpernel livery of two-tone red. Eventually even the word 'Blue' was dropped and the vehicles bore the name 'Scarlet Coaches'.

Trading continued through into the 1960s, but the rapid increase in private car ownership was greatly affecting the number of people using buses and coaches. Bill and Jack Hawkins were now over the usual retirement age and so, in April 1966, part of the business was sold to Mr Douggie Venner, then proprietor of Venner's Tours at Witheridge in Devon but originally a thatcher by trade. He continued with a programme of tours and excursions from

Minehead, using the name 'Scarlet Coaches', and his family continued to serve the travelling public in the Minehead area until 1997, when the business was sold to Southern National. The remainder of the Scarlet and Blue fleet was sold off.

The Hawkins brothers went into a well-earned retirement after some 46 years in the coach business. They will always be remembered by those who took their holidays in, or were resident at, Minehead. Countless former passengers will have abiding memories of happy days out in the immaculately presented, gleaming two-tone red coaches of a family firm which served the travelling public well for so long.

The End of an Era

It would be a very courageous person who even attempted to look into the future and predict the form and role that public transport will take in the twenty-first century. At the beginning of the twentieth century, when the motor car was in its primitive form, who could have foreseen the remarkable changes that would take place in all types of transport within the space of a hundred years? It is a century which has seen the development of the bus and coach, bringing freedom to travel for a population which had never moved far from the immediate vicinity of their town or village. The popularity of coaches and buses reached its zenith immediately after the Second World War, then went into an irreversible decline. Now, with a population firmly wedded to the

By the 1960s coaches were having to compete with the rapid growth in private car ownership. This picture, which dates from around 1970, shows coaches competing for road space outside the Old Nunnery in Dunster. (EPA)

private car, recovery to anything approaching its peak is beyond the industry's reach.

This century has also witnessed the development of personal transport from the first few motor vehicles (typically preceded by a man carrying a red flag) to a level of car ownership that has brought problems of congestion, accidents, pollution and environmental damage. The conflict between the demand for travel without restriction and a desperate need for constraint seems irreconcilable. In spite of various attempts to find a new role for public transport, the continued popularity of personal transport is simply overwhelming.

It is useful to look back over history to see what lessons can be learned. In the nineteenth century the railways played a key role during the industrial revolution. Likewise the bus and coach emerged only to decline within the middle decades of the twentieth century, when it had fulfilled its role as a means of mass travel. This implies that simply tinkering with outmoded forms of transport is likely to be doomed to failure. Some contemporary efforts to do so may seem as ludicrous to the citizens of the future as the man with the red flag does to us today. History suggests that human ingenuity will find the solution in environmentally sustainable transport. What form this will take is impossible to predict.

Nevertheless, for those who were involved in the development of public transport, the late nineteenth and early twentieth centuries were a period of excitement. It added an important dimension to the freedom of the population, not only as part of the social history of the time, but also in the development of Minehead and the other Exmoor communities as holiday resorts.

Appendix A

COACHES OPERATED BY HAWKINS BROTHERS,
SCARLET PIMPERNEL AND SCARLET AND BLUE COACHES LTD

Reg. No.	Chassis Make	Body Make	Seats	New	Bought	Sold
-?-	Rolls Royce	not known	14	no details known		
YA2858	Fiat	not known	14	1922	Mar. 1922	by 1930
YA4650	Lancia Z	not known	14	1923	Jan. 1923	by 1931
YC22	Lancia Z	not known	20	1927	June 1927	July 1933
YC3111	Lancia Z	not known	20	1928	May 1928	Mar. 1934
YC5676	Graham-Dodge	not known	14	1929	Mar. 1929	June 1936
YC6222	Reo	Eaton	20	1929	May 1929	Oct. 1936
—9078	no details available					
YD4771	Leyland Cub	Mumford	20	1932	May 1932	Oct. 1936
YD5110	Bedford WLB	Duple	20	1932	July 1932	June 1936
YD7356	Leyland Cub	Beadle	26	1933	June 1933	Mar. 1942
YD9811	Leyland Cub	Beadle	26	1934	May 1934	Feb. 1946
AYA102	Dennis Ace	Harrington	20	1934	June 1934	Oct. 1937
YO9167	no details known					
AYC926*	Leyland Lion	Duple	32	1935	May 1935	May 1951
AYD43	Bedford WTL	Duple	20	1935	June 1935	Nov. 1938
YD4700	Dennis Dart	Duple	20	1932	May 1936	Oct. 1936
BYC675	Leyland Cub	Duple	25	1936	May 1936	Mar. 1950
BYC785	Leyland Cub	Beadle	26	1936	June 1936	May 1950
CYB500	Bedford WTB	Duple	25	1937	Feb. 1937	May 1946
CYB774	Albion Victor	Harrington	26	1937	Mar. 1937	Jan. 1950
CYC375	Leyland Cub	Duple	26	1937	May. 1937	April 1951
DYB453	Leyland Cub	Beadle	25	1938	April 1938	May 1950
DYB645	Leyland Lion	not known	32	1938	April 1938	Sept. 1939
DYC21	Bedford WTB	Duple	25	1938	June 1938	Jan. 1949
EYC296	Leyland Lion	Harrington	28	1939	July 1939	Mar. 1952
FYD81	Bedford OWB	Duple	32	1942	Dec. 1942	1946
GYB531	Bedford OB	Duple	32	1945	Oct. 1945	not known
EYB444*	Leyland Cheetah	Harrington	31	1939	1945	Mar. 1953
KYA582	Dennis Lancet	Harrington	33	1948	Aug. 1948	Jan. 1960
JYD95	Leyland Tiger	Duple	33	1949	Feb. 1949	June 1960
KYC217	Daimler CVD6	Beadle	32	1949	Mar. 1949	Oct. 1960
KYC926	Bedford OB	Duple	27	1949	Mar. 1949	April 1954
KYD151	AEC Regal 3	Harrington	33	1949	Mar. 1949	May 1962

LYC462	Albion Victor	Duple	29	1950	April 1950	June 1958
LYC691	Leyland Tiger	Harrington	33	1950	April 1950	April 1962
MYA590	Leyland Comet	Harrington	29	1950	July 1950	March 1966
MYC801	Bedford OB	Duple	27	1951	April 1951	June 1958
NYA378	Commer Avenger	Harrington	28	1951	June 1951	April 1966
NYD578	Bedford SB	Duple	33	1952	May 1952	Nov. 1965
OYA616	Bedford SB	Harrington	31	1952	June 1952	March 1966
PYB256	Bedford SB	Duple	35	1953	June 1953	April 1966
CYB715‡	Leyland Lion	Harrington	31	1937	April 1954	May 1954
JYC855‡	Leyland Tiger	Harrington	33	1948	April 1954	April 1960
JYD199‡	Leyland Tiger	Harrington	33	1948	April 1954	Sept. 1959
LYD581‡	Leyland Comet	Harrington	29	1950	April 1954	Oct. 1963
MYA121‡	Leyland Tiger	Burlingham	33	1950	April 1954	July 1958
MYA246‡	Leyland Comet	Harrington	29	1950	April 1954	April 1963
NYC993‡	Bedford SB	Duple	31	1952	April 1954	Aug. 1965
PYA973‡	Bedford SB	Harrington	33	1953	April 1954	May 66
PYB383‡	Bedford SB	Duple	35	1953	April 1954	Mar. 66
748BYB	Bedford SB3	Duple	41	1958	July 1958	May 1966
597HYD	Bedford SB3	Duple	41	1960	July 1960	May 1966
498PYB	Bedford SB5	Duple	41	1962	June 1962	April 1966
135TYC	Bedford SB5	Duple	41	1963	June 1963	May 1966

Notes

* AYC926 was requisitioned during the Second World War, being returned to Hawkins Brothers in December 1945. EYB444 was requisitioned when new and returned to Hawkins Brothers in 1945.

‡Vehicles acquired from Porlock Blue Motors on the formation of Scarlet and Blue Coaches.

All coaches were bought new except YD5110, Vauxhall Motors demonstration chassis, and YD4700, from Hobbs Brothers, Minehead.

Appendix B

JONES'S
COACHING & MOTOR TRIPS

FROM LYNTON.

The well-appointed
LORNA DOONE
and RED DEER

MOTOR Chars-a-banc RUN DAILY during the Summer Months to

MINEHEAD.

"LORNA" runs from 29th March to 30th October.
"RED DEER" runs from 5th April to 30th October

"LORNA" Motor Char-a-banc leaves LYNTON and LYNMOUTH at 10 a.m. daily (Sundays excepted) arriving at Minehead Station at 11.15 a.m. for the 12.50 train. Single Fare 10/-. Return 18/-.

"RED DEER" leaves LYNTON & LYNMOUTH at 3.30 p.m., via Watersmeet, Brendon, Malmsmead (for Doone Valley) arriving 4.15 p.m. at Malmsmead, staying 45 minutes for tea, and arrive in Minehead at 6.45. Considered the finest drive in the British Isles. Fare 10/-.

Through Carriages from Minehead to Paddington.

A
CHAR-A-BANC
runs daily at 11 a.m. to

DOONE VALLEY.

The Route descends the West Lyn Valley to Lynmouth, and along the wooded slopes of Summer House Hill to Watersmeet, thence by Coombe Park water to Ilford Bridge, where Farley Water is crossed; a steep rise climbed, and descending by Brendon Church the most beautiful riverine and hill scenery is met with, passing successively Rockford, Millslade, Brendon, and Malmsmead, whence the Doone Valley is reached, and where refreshments may be had for man and beast. Return at 3.30 past the reputed residence of John Ridd, the Church in which Lorna Doone was married, and rising to a height of 1,000 feet, home by the grand coast scenery of Countisbury. Fare 7/6.

A
CHAR-A-BANC
runs daily at 11 a.m. to

HUNTER'S INN via Woody Bay
FOR HEDDONSMOUTH.

A drive unequalled in Devon for bold seascapes and wooded landscapes. Via Winter Top (about 1,100 feet high) over the far-famed Martinhoe Common to the Heddon Valley, and the excellent appointment of the Hunter's Inn. At 3.30 the "Exmoor" returns by Heddon Valley, Parracombe, and the West Lyn, to Lynton. Three hours allowed at Hunter's Inn. Fare 7/6.

A Char-a-banc
runs DAILY at 11 a.m. to

SIMONSBATH.

Through Watersmeet Valley to Brendon Church, then passing Brendon Barton, a turn is made to the left, and the moorland in its naked grandeur is before us. Some miles of this majestic scenery brings us to the head waters of the Exe, ascending from which we then drop gently down to the waters of the Barle, and enter the beautifully wooded surroundings of the village of Simonsbath. At 3.30 p.m. the return journey begins, and 5.30 p.m. again finds us in Lynton. Fare 7/6.

Motor Char-a-banc

DEPART	ARRIVE
LYNTON (Coach Office) 10 a.m.	ILFRACOMBE 11.30 a.m.
ILFRACOMBE 4 p.m.	LYNTON (Coach Office) 5.30 p.m.

To ILFRACOMBE.

The Route is through Barbrook and ascending Dean Steep to Woody Bay Station we are 1,100 feet above sea level. To the right we see the beautiful valley leading down to Hunter's Inn and Heddons Mouth. The descent to Parracombe and the ascent the other side afford a grand panoramic view of the village and surrounding country and brings us to Blackmore Gate, where an old Toll Gate formerly stood. Continuing we come to the village of Combe Martin with the old Parish Church on the left. Thence we traverse some of the best coast scenery in the county as we approach Watermouth Castle with its noted caves and splendid landscape views. A short run further, and looming in the distance we see Ilfracombe Harbour, and rising from the waters edge the town surmounted as it were by the lovely Tors Walk.
FARE 12/-.

Motor Char-a-banc
runs Daily to

Leaving the Coach Office at 9.45 a.m.

CLOVELLY, "The quaintest Village in the Kingdom."

The Route is via Parracombe and Blackmore Gate, as in the Ilfracombe trip. On reaching the old Turn-pike at Blackmoor the Barnstaple road is taken with its varied and beautiful scenery. Passing through Barnstaple and Instow with Appledore on our right we arrive at Bideford, and cross its noted bridge. After a halt of 15 minutes we continue and arrive at Clovelly at 12.45 p.m. This quaint village, built on the side of the Cliff, consists of one street in a series of broad stairs, necessitating the use of donkeys as pack animals for the conveyance of goods up and to draw sleighs down. At 3 p.m. the return is made to Barnstaple where half-an-hour is allowed for tea, and then on to Blackmoor, Parracombe and Woody Bay, arriving home at 6.30 p.m. with very pleasant recollections of our 85 miles tour. Fare £1.

Private Carriages or Cars (Open or Closed) to meet any train at Lynton, Barnstaple, Minehead or Ilfracombe on receipt of Wire. Telegrams—Tom Jones, Lynton. Telephone—No. 2, Lynton. Agent for Lynton & Barnstaple Railway. Furniture Removed and Stored

Chars-a-banc run to the Meets of Devon and Somerset Stag Hounds at Cloutsham, Yearnor Moor, Brendon Two Gates, Hawkcombe Head, &c. Devonshire Cobs for Hunting or Hacking. Horses for Driving by day or job.

BOOK SEATS AT
Jones's Coach Office

CHURCH HILL, LYNTON. ('Phone—Lynton 2.)

POWERFUL MOTOR CARS ON HIRE WITH EXPERIENCED DRIVERS.

TOM JONES, Coach Proprietor, Lynton.

CLARKE, Printer, Lynton.

AFTERNOON TOURS

DAILY (including Sunday)

		Fares.
Start 2.30 p.m. Home approx. 7 p.m.	**LYNMOUTH and EXMOOR** Via PORLOCK, returning via SIMONSBATH and EXFORD.	5/- Child 2/6
Start 2.30 p.m. Home approx. 7 p.m.	**TARR STEPS** Via WINSFORD, WINSFORD HILL, and DULVERTON, returning via the EXE VALLEY.	5/- Child 2/6
Start 2.30 p.m. Home approx. 6.45 p.m.	**DOONE VALLEY and OARE CHURCH**	4/- Child 2/-
Start 2.30 p.m. Home approx. 6.30 p.m.	**OVER DUNKERY** Via Wheddon Cross, Dunkery Hill Gate, and HORNER WOODS. Allowing time for Tea at Horner.	3/6 Child 2/-
Start 2.30 p.m. Home approx. 7 p.m.	**OVER EXMOOR** Via EXFORD, HAWKCOMBE HEAD, CHETSFORD WATER and PORLOCK for Tea. Returning via BOSSINGTON.	4/- Child 2/-
Start 2.30 p.m. Home approx. 6.30 p.m.	**QUANTOCK HILLS** Via BLUE ANCHOR, WATCHET, HOLFORD GLEN, for Tea. Returning via Crowcombe.	4/6 Child 2/6
Start 2.30 p.m. Home approx. 7 p.m.	**Grand New MOORLAND TOUR** Via WINSFORD, WITHYPOOL, SANDYWAY, MOLLAND MOOR, DULVERTON (for Tea), returning via BURY HILL and HEATHPOULT.	5/- Child 2/6
Start 2.30 p.m. Home approx. 6.15 p.m.	**SELWORTHY** PORLOCK and PORLOCK WEIR, returning via BOSSINGTON. Allowing time at Porlock for Tea.	2/6 Child 1/6
Start 2.30 p.m. Home approx. 7 p.m.	**LYNMOUTH, DOONE VALLEY and OARE CHURCH** Allowing time at Brendon for Tea.	5/- Child 2/6
Start 2.30 p.m. Home approx. 6.45 p.m.	SPECIAL HALF-DAY TO **COTHELSTONE** Via WILLITON, NETHER STOWEY, returning via BISHOP'S LYDEARD and MONKSILVER.	5/- Child 2/6

Scarlet Pimpernel

OBSERVATION COACHES

TEL. 78.

From MINEHEAD and ALCOMBE

Wookey Hole Caves.

		Fares.
DAILY Start 10 a.m. Home approx. 7 p.m.	ALL-DAY TOUR TO **WOOKEY HOLE CAVES** AND **Cheddar Caves** Via GLASTONBURY, WELLS, & CHEDDAR GORGE. Allowing ½ hour at Glastonbury, 1½ hours at Wookey, ¾ hour at Wells, and 1 hour at Cheddar.	8/- Child 4/-
DAILY Start 10.15 a.m. Home approx. 6.30 p.m.	ALL-DAY TOUR TO **LYNMOUTH** RETURNING VIA **WATERSMEET** BRENDON **DOONE VALLEY** AND **OARE CHURCH** Allowing 2¼ hours at Lynmouth, ½ hour at Watersmeet, 1½ hours at Doone Valley.	6/- Child 3/-
DAILY Start 10 a.m. Home approx. 7 p.m.	ALL-DAY TOUR TO **GLASTONBURY ABBEY WELLS CATHEDRAL** AND **CHEDDAR CAVES & GORGE** Via QUANTOCK HILLS, BRIDGWATER and POLDEN HILLS, returning via AXBRIDGE, EAST BRENT, and BRIDGWATER. Allowing half-hour at Glastonbury, 2 hours at Wells, 1 hour at Cheddar.	8/- Child 4/-

		Fares.
DAILY Start 9.30 a.m. Home approx. 7 p.m. (Sundays excepted)	ALL-DAY TOUR TO **CLOVELLY** Via SIMONSBATH, BRAYFORD, AND BARNSTAPLE, returning via BIDEFORD, SOUTHMOLTON, and EXE VALLEY.	9/- Child 4/6
DAILY Start 10 a.m. Home approx. 6.45 p.m.	ALL-DAY TOUR TO **ILFRACOMBE** Via LYNMOUTH and COMBE MARTIN, returning over EXMOOR and SIMONSBATH. Allowing ½ hour at Lynmouth and 3 hours at Ilfracombe.	7/6 Child 4/-
MONDAY WEDNESDAY AND FRIDAY Start 9.30 a.m. Home approx. 7.15 p.m.	ALL-DAY TOUR TO **TORQUAY** With beautiful Circular Drive beyond EXETER, via Starcross, DAWLISH, and TEIGNMOUTH (Coast Road), returning via EXETER and EXE VALLEY. Allowing 2 hours at Torquay and 1 hour at Exeter.	8/6 Child 4/6
TUESDAY THURSDAY AND SATURDAY Start 10 a.m. Home approx. 6.45 p.m.	ALL-DAY CIRCULAR TOUR TO **SIDMOUTH** Via TAUNTON and HONITON, returning via EXETER, TIVERTON, and EXE VALLEY. Allowing 2 hours at Sidmouth and 1 hour at Exeter.	7/- Child 3/6
TUESDAY & THURSDAY Start 10.15 a.m. Home approx. 6.30 p.m.	**LYNMOUTH (Direct) AND LYNTON** Allowing 5 hours at Lynmouth and Lynton.	5/6 Child 3/-
MONDAY TUESDAY THURSDAY AND SATURDAY Start 10 a.m. Home approx. 6.30 p.m.	ALL-DAY CIRCULAR TOUR **OVER EXMOOR** Via Porlock, LYNMOUTH, WATERSMEET, Simonsbath, WINSFORD HILL, TARR STEPS, Dulverton, Exe Valley, and Dunster. Allowing 2 hours at Lynmouth, ½ hour at Watersmeet, ½ hour at Tarr Steps, 1 hour at Dulverton.	7/6 Child 4/-
MONDAY WEDNESDAY AND FRIDAY Start 9 a.m. Home approx. 7.45 p.m.	ALL-DAY CIRCULAR TOUR **OVER DARTMOOR** Via BOVEY TRACEY, WIDECOMBE IN THE MOOR, TWO BRIDGES, PRINCETOWN, MORETON HAMPSTEAD and EXETER.	10/- Child 5/-

		Fares.
TUESDAY AND FRIDAY Start 9.30 a.m. Home approx. 7 p.m.	ALL-DAY TOUR TO **BUCKFAST ABBEY & Exeter** Allowing 2 hours at Buckfast and 1 hour at Exeter.	7/6 Child 4/-
WEDNESDAY Start 10 a.m. Home approx. 6.45 p.m.	ALL-DAY TOUR TO **HUNTERS INN and WOOLACOMBE SANDS** Via LYNMOUTH, returning via SIMONSBATH and EXFORD. Allowing 1½ hours at Hunters Inn and ¾ hour at Woolacombe. Tea at Blackmore Gate.	8/6 Child 4/6
TUESDAY THURSDAY & SATURDAY Start 10 a.m. Home approx. 7 p.m.	ALL-DAY TOUR TO **LYME REGIS** Via TAUNTON and CHARD, returning HONITON, TIVERTON, and EXE VALLEY. Allowing 2 hours at Lyme Regis and 1 hour at Tiverton.	7/- Child 3/6
WEDNESDAY & FRIDAY Start 9.30 a.m. Home approx. 7.15 p.m.	ALL-DAY TOUR TO **EXETER** Via TIVERTON and Exe Valley.	6/- Child 3/-
SATURDAY Start 10 a.m. Home approx. 6.30 p.m.	ALL-DAY TOUR TO **WESTON-SUPER-MARE** Allowing 5 hours at Weston-super-Mare.	6/- Child 3/-
FRIDAY Start 10 a.m. Home approx. 6.45 p.m.	ALL-DAY TOUR TO **DAWLISH & TEIGNMOUTH** Via EXETER, returning via TIVERTON and EXE VALLEY. Allowing ½ hour at Dawlish and 2 hours at Teignmouth.	7/- Child 3/6
TUESDAY & THURSDAY Start 10 a.m. Home approx. 6.45 p.m.	ALL-DAY TOUR TO **EXMOUTH** Via TAUNTON and HONITON, returning via EXETER and EXE VALLEY. Allowing 2 hours at Exmouth and 1 hour at Exeter.	7/- Child 3/6

AFTERNOON TOURS (continued)

		Fares.
DAILY Start 2.30 p.m. (Sundays excepted) Home approx. 6.30 p.m.	**OVER BRENDON HILL** Returning via CLEEVE ABBEY, OLD CLEEVE, and BLUE ANCHOR. Allowing time for Tea at Cleeve Abbey.	**3/6** Child 2/-
SUNDAY Start 2.30 p.m. Home approx. 7.30 p.m.	**HALF-DAY TOUR TO CHEDDAR CAVES** Returning via Axbridge and Bridgwater. Allowing 1½ hours at Cheddar.	**5/-** Child 2/6
SUNDAY Start 2.30 p.m. Home approx. 7.30 p.m.	**HALF-DAY TOUR TO WOOKEY HOLE CAVES** Via GLASTONBURY, and WELLS. Allowing 1½ hours at Wookey.	**5/-** Child 2/-
SUNDAY Start 2.30 p.m. Home approx. 7.30 p.m.	**HALF-DAY TOUR TO WESTON-SUPER-MARE** Allowing 2 hours at Weston.	**5/-** Child 2/6

EVENING TOURS
DAILY (including Sunday)

Start 7 p.m.	**OVER DUNKERY and HORNER WOODS**	**2/-** Child 1/-
Start 7 p.m.	**CROYDON HILLS and LUXBOROUGH VALLEY**	**2/-** Child 1/-
Start 7 p.m.	**SELWORTHY, BOSSINGTON, PORLOCK and HORNER WOODS**	**1/6** Child 1/-
Start 7 p.m.	**St. AUDRIES, WATCHET and BLUE ANCHOR**	**1/6** Child 1/-
Start 7 p.m.	**BRENDON HILL**	**2/6** Child 1/6
Start 7 p.m.	**DUNSTER, WOOTTON COURTENAY and LUCCOMBE**	**1/6** Child 1/-

Tours are also operated in connection with Meets of Hounds to the following points :—

	Adult	Child		Adult	Child
CLOUTSHAM ...	3/6	2/-	ALDERMAN'S		
HELE BRIDGE ...	4/-	2/-	BARROW	4/-	2/-
HEATHPOULT ...	3/6	2/-	LARK BARROW	4/-	2/-
MOUNTSEY HILL	4/-	2/-	DUNSTER ...	4/-	2/-
STOWEY	3/6	2/-	WEBBER'S POST	3/6	2/-
WHEDDON CROSS	3/6	2/-	CHILLY BRIDGE	4/-	2/-
WINSFORD ...	3/6	2/-	COUNTY GATE ...	4/-	2/-
BRENDON TWO GATES	5/-	2/6	RALEIGH CROSS	3/6	2/-
COMER'S GATE ...	4/-	2/-	St. AUDRIES ...	2/6	1/6
DUNKERY HILL GATE	3/6	2/-	COTHELSTONE ...	4/-	2/-
EXFORD ...	3/6	2/-	CROWCOMBE ...	3/6	2/-
HAWKCOMBE HEAD	3/6	2/-	FAIRFIELD ...	4/-	2/-
HADDON ...	4/6	2/6	HOLFORD ...	3/6	2/-
			CASTLE COMFORT	3/6	2/-

SPECIAL RATES FOR PRIVATE PARTIES.

Special Tours will be run each week to other places of interest, particulars of which can be obtained at Booking Offices.

BOOKING OFFICES :—

Main Booking Office—Adjoining West Somerset Cafe, The Avenue, (opposite Woolworth's Stores).

Adjoining " Allenhayes," The Avenue. Sea Front.

BRANCH BOOKING OFFICES.

" Como," Alcombe Road, Alcombe.

Adjoining Ann's Pantry, Alcombe Road, Alcombe.

Proprietors—HAWKINS BROS., Feathers Yard, Minehead.

TERMS AND CONDITIONS UNDER WHICH TOURS ARE RUN.

The Company reserve the right to cancel any advertised Tour should there be insufficient passengers, to alter the route of any Tour and time of departure should circumstances demand, but the times and routes will be adhered to as far as possible.

Although every endeavour will be made by the Proprietors to keep the seats marked off there is no guarantee given or implied.

COX, PRINTERS, MINEHEAD.

(Left and above) The complete programme of Scarlet Pimpernel Tours (c.1939).

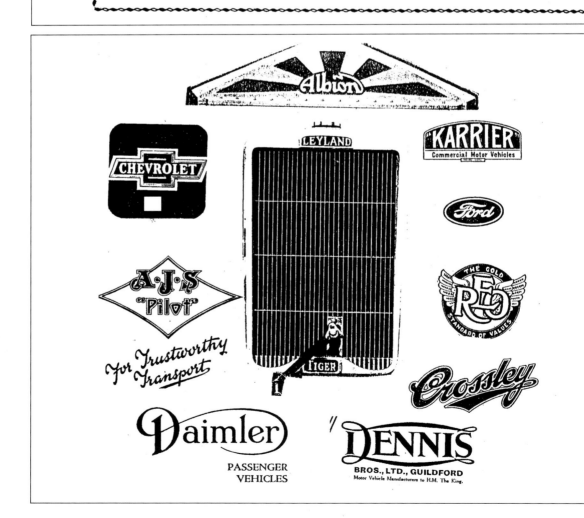

LYNTON, NORTH DEVON.

Royal Castle

FAMILY HOTEL.

Patronised by

H.R.H. the Prince of Wales,

And other Members of the

Royal Family.

THE FINEST SEA AND LAND VIEWS IN THE WORLD.

THIS HOTEL, standing in its own Ornamental Grounds of about 70 Acres, 500 feet above the level of the Sea, overlooking the Bristol Channel, commands uninterrupted views of the Valleys of the East and West Lynn, Lynn Cliff, Brendon and Countisbury Hills, The Tors, the Village of Lynmouth, the Foreland, the Welsh Coast, and the far-famed Valley of Rocks.

Having been under the management of the present Proprietor for nearly 50 Years, the Hotel has been recently and extensively enlarged to meet the requirements of modern society, and combines the comfort of a Private House with the conveniences of a First-class Hotel.

Elegant Suites of Private Apartments, Table d'Hôte, Coffee Room, and Ladies' Drawing Room, to which have been added, this season, New and Commodious Smoking and Billiard Rooms, all facing the Sea. Excellent Cuisine. Moderate Charges.

Shooting (Black Cock and other Game) for Gentlemen staying at the Hotel only. Salmon and Trout Fishing.

LAWN TENNIS.

FIRST-CLASS STABLING.

POST HORSES AND CARRIAGES OF EVERY DESCRIPTION

Coaches in the Season to Ilfracombe, Minehead, and Barnstaple.

—— TARIFF ON APPLICATION. ——

THOMAS BAKER, PROPRIETOR.

EXMOOR PONIES FOR SALE.

Subscribers

Mrs M. Ackland, Taunton, Somerset
Patrick Adams, Dulverton, Somerset
Canon Ian Ainsworth-Smith, Milverton, Somerset
Mrs V. Anand, Mitcham, Surrey
P.T.K. Anderson, Wisborough Green, West Sussex
J.A. Atkin, Withypool, Minehead, Somerset
Roger Atkinson O.B.E., Chester
Martyn Babb, Blue Anchor, Nr. Minehead, Somerset
Bridget Baillie, Dulverton, Somerset
Miss Annabel G. Bain, London W8
Mrs Sylvia Baker, Exwick, Exeter, Devon
J. Bamsey
Mr D.R. Barber, Sidmouth, Devon
Mr G.W. Barker, Durham
D.M. Barwell, Droitwich Spa, Worcs
Graham Batten - Joint owner of Scarlet Pimpernel
   Leyland Comet MYA 590
Mrs S.G. Beale, Tiverton, Devon
Mr Allan Bruce Bedford, Erith, Kent
Mr J.P. Bennett, Loughborough, Leics
Sally Best, Longbridge, Deverill
Mrs Wendy Bibby, West Baldwin, Isle of Man
Ken Biggs, Camerton, Bath
Colin Billington, Fifield, Maidenhead, Berks
Victor Bonham-Carter, Milverton, Somerset
Gerhard Borchert, Ludweigshaten, Germany
Mr and Mrs C.H. Bowden, Minehead, Somerset
A.J. Boyce, Torquay, Devon
Mrs Jenny Bray, Farnham, Surrey
Mr G.W.K. Broadhurst, Feniton, Devon
Alan D. Broughall, Neston, South Wirral
James E. Brown, Saffron Walden, Essex
Mr John F. Brown, Weymouth, Dorset
T.C. Bryant, Maes Y Crynwyr, Llwngwril
Mr D.J. Bubier, Newport, Gwent
Mr and Mrs R.I. Buick, Minehead, Somerset
David Burch, Westlea, Swindon, Wilts
G.H. Burnell, Wootton Courtenay
K.J. Burrow, Bucks Cross, Bideford, Devon
Mr and Mrs R.J. Butcher, Dulverton, Somerset
Christopher A.J. Cann, Coleford, Devon
Prof. Roger Carey, Pollokshields, Glasgow
W.J. Carman, St. Sampson's, Guernsey, C.I.
Jack and Chris Carter, Nailsworth
Peter Carter, Porlock, Somerset
Elaine and David Chant, Walmley, Sutton Coldfield
Sally Chilcott, Westbury, Wilts
John Clarke, Melton Mowbray, Leics
Fraser Clayton, Baynards, Sussex
J.R.G. Cobbett, Denmead, Hampshire
Brian Gordon Coe, Kettering, Northants

Mr A.A. Collins, Saughall, Chester
Mrs J.M. Cook, Cheltenham, Glos
Mr K.I. Cook, Watchet, Somerset
Mr C.D. Corner, Porlock, Somerset
Bob Cornish, Newton Abbot, Devon
Mr Mervyn Cornish, Watchet, Somerset
Miss Valerie A. Couch, Taunton, Somerset
Robert Crawley, Colaton Raleigh, Devon
Mrs Barbara D. Crippen, Stanmore, Middx
Philip Croshaw, Sark, Channel Isles
J.M. Cummings, Edgware, Middx
Oliver Davies, London
Mr C.J. Davis, Malvern, Worcs
Robert C. Davis, Poole, Dorset
Stephen Dear, Minehead, Somerset
Rowland P. Dell, Wootton Courtenay, Somerset
Mr Terence A.G. Dendy
Glenys and David Dunworth, West Wickham, Kent
Margaret Beryl Dutton, Pensilva, Cornwall
Mr Chris Dyer, Minehead, Somerset
M. Earl, Ewell, Surrey
N.J. Earl, Farnham, Surrey
K. Eastham
Gerry Eddolls, Porlock, Somerset
Prof. Alec Eden, Torquay, Devon
Mrs A.G. Eggar, Timberscombe, Minehead
Christopher B. Ellis, North Kelvinside, Glasgow
Mrs J.M. Evans, Wellington, Somerset
The Exmoor Society, Dulverton, Somerset
W.H.A. Eyles, Crediton, Devon
Brian G. Finch, Caterham, Surrey
Richard Ford, Horsell, Woking, Surrey
Mrs J.R. Fraser, Colyton, Devon
Mr Laurence Fricker and Miss Flora Fricker, Southsea,
   Hants
Mr R.H. Gadsby, Liversedge, W. Yorks.
G.B. Gamble, Horner, Somerset
Bryan and Peggy George, Leyland
Miss C.J. Giddens, Minehead, Somerset
D.S. Giles, Westcliff-on-Sea, Essex
P.H. Gill, Portishead, Bristol
Mr G.W. Glover, Wembworthy, Chulmleigh, Devon
Mrs Margaret Gould, Minehead, Somerset
Ian Grainger, Enstone, Chipping Norton, Oxon
Mr R.E. Gray, Fareham, Hants
Robert Green, Minehead, Somerset
Mr I.J. Greenfield, Yelvertoft, Northants
J.R. Greenland, Weston-super-Mare, Somerset
Monica and Peter Grimley, Epsom, Surrey
Mr D.C. Grimmett, Minehead, Somerset
R.O. Hancock, Taunton, Somerset

R.N. Hannay, Goostrey, Crewe

A.D. Hanson, Lindley, Huddersfield

Andrew Harding, Egerton, Bolton

Peter G. Harding, London

Yvonne and Philip Harland, Kings Langley, Herts.

Don Harrison, Dagenham, Essex

C. Hartwright, Abingdon, Oxon

Mr J.M. Hawes, Enfield, Middlesex

Alan Hawkins, Oakwood, Derby

Lyndsey Hawkins, Stokeinteignhead, Devon

Malcolm Hawkins, Plymouth, Devon

Richard Hawkins, Oakwood, Derby

Robin and Maureen Hawkins, Alcombe, Minehead,
    Somerset

Suzanne Hawkins, Crookes, Sheffield

L.W. Henderson, Southgate, London N14

Mr P. Brian Hicks, Cookham, Maidenhead, Berks.

C.R. Higgins, Bognor Regis, West Sussex

E.W. Higham, Wigan, Lancs

Mr S. Hillman, Barnstaple, Devon

Dale Hitchman, Charlton Marshall, Blandford, Dorset

Richard S. Hobbs, East Budleigh, Devon

Paul Hodder-Williams, Beaconsfield, Bucks.

Peter H. Hollands, Malvern Wells, Worcs.

Mr M.J. Hopkins, Taunton, Somerset

Caroline and David Horne, Wellington Heath,
    Herefordshire

Mr E. Hudson, Marton, Blackpool

Christopher P. Humphries, Launceston, Cornwall

D.S. Hunter, Wells, Somerset

David Hurley

Revd J.W. Hurrell, Porlock, Somerset

. Ingram, Griffithstown, Gwent

Neil Jennings, Paulton, Bristol

Malcolm Johnson, Horsham, West Sussex

D.M. Jones, Hove, East Sussex

Mrs Joyce Jones, South Molton, Devon

Mrs Toni Jones, Dulverton, Somerset

K.D. Jubb, Redditch, Worcs.

Michael Kennard

Pam Kennard, Gerrards Cross, Bucks.

Arthur Kingdom, Tiverton, Devon

D.M. Kirby, Alfrick, Worcester

Mrs S.A. Knifton, Bexhill-on-Sea, East Sussex

Roger Langrish, Wootton Courtenay, Somerset

Stuart Lawrence , Minehead, Somerset

Paul and Nancy Lefevre, Oakham, Rutland

Barry Le Jeune, Haywards Heath, W. Sussex

Richard Lethbridge, Umberleigh, Devon

Colin J. N. Lindsey, Ickleton, Cambridgeshire

Helen Lonsdale, Drayton Beauchamp, Aylesbury,
    Bucks

Mr K.R. Love, Lower Earley, Reading, Berks

Mr H. Luff, London SE24

Mrs J. Maguire, Dunlaoghaire, Co. Dublin

Dr John Malin, Minehead, Somerset

Dennis and Mollie Martin, Exeter, Devon

Michael J. Meilton, Chippenham, Wilts.

G.C. Merrifield, Taunton, Somerset

Mrs C. Mitchell, Shepton Mallet, Somerset

Mrs Madge Money, Bedford

Mrs Olive Moody, Minehead, Somerset

Mr J.A. Moore, Taunton, Somerset

R.I.J. Morgan, Luton, Beds.

M.T. Morgan, Highbridge, Somerset

Peter Morley, Coulsdon

P.H. Mountford, Royston, Herts.

Mr A.A. Munro, Sandhurst, Berks.

Alan Nightingale, Sidmouth, Devon

Miss C.M. Norris, West Harracott, Barnstaple, Devon

H.A. Norris, King's Lynn, Norfolk

Christopher Norrish, Clevedon, Somerset

J.G.E. Nye, Garstang, Lancs.

Mrs T.A. Page, Chigwell, Essex

A.J. Parsons, Horsham, West Sussex

R.B. Partridge, Chelmsford, Essex

Mrs J.D. Payne, Westbury, Wilts.

D.M. Persson, Enfield, Middx.

Dr Hugh Pincott, Frome

J.F. Platt, Sutton Coldfield, W. Midlands

Mr D.R. Poole, Timberscombe, Minehead, Somerset

Mr R.B. Poole, Barnstaple, Devon

Colin Prince - Joint owner of Scarlet Pimpernel
    Leyland Comet MYA 590, Stoneleigh, Epsom, Surrey

Lieutenant-Commander J.A.F. Pugsley - Royal Navy,
    Plympton-St-Maurice, South Devon

Mr E.A. Purchase, Hitchin, Herts.

Mr N. Randall, Leighton Buzzard

Mr David Rawle, Minehead, Somerset

Mrs R.A. Rendell, Exeter, Devon

Mr J.C. Reynolds, Goring-by-Sea, Worthing, West
    Sussex

Mr A. Richings, Plymouth, Devon

Gordon Richmond, Bristol

Andrew M. Roberts, Yardley, Birmingham

Les Ronan, Cheselbourne, Dorchester, Dorset

Paul L. Rouet, Winchester, Hants.

Mr Eric Rowlands, Luccombe, Minehead, Somerset

Mr John L. Rugg, Laindon, Basildon, Essex

Mrs D. Sage, Porlock, Somerset

David Salter

Mrs Valerie Samoilys

John Sampson, South Molton, N. Devon

Michael Scarlett, Williton, Somerset

M.J. Scott, Minehead, Somerset

Prue and Lawrie Scott, Barnstaple, Devon

Mr C.P. Sharp, Maulden, Beds.

Mr R.A. Shaw, Chellaston, Derby

C.T. Shears, Chulmleigh, Devon

S.R. Shelton, Tettenhall, Wolverhampton

M.H. Shilson, London, NW2

Roy Shopland, West Hill, Ottery St Mary, Devon

Frank D. Simpson, Llanvair Kilgeddin, Abergavenny

Anne and Bob Smith, Tiverton, Devon

Mark Smith, Halesowen, West Midlands
Alan Smithers, Haslemere, Surrey
Frederick A. Smyth, Edgware, Middx.
Andrew Spriggs, Greetland, Halifax, W. Yorks.
Terrence Squire, Barnstaple, Devon
John Stanley, Ilkley, West Yorkshire
M.J. Stephens, Lightwater, Surrey
Carol Stokes, Basingstoke, Hampshire
Mr M.A. Storr, Tiverton, Devon
Mrs Sheila Sutton, Hawkcombe, Porlock, Minehead
Sue and Robert Sutton, Ledbury, Herefordshire
Mrs M. Tarr, Langford Budville, Wellington, Somerset
J. Taylor, Leigh-on-Sea, Essex
R.N. Thomas, Abberley, Worcester
J.D. Thorne, Newport, Gwent
L.J. Tincknell, Marlborough, Wilts.
Mr and Mrs Peter Tout, Witheridge, Devon
M.J. Tozer, Pill, Bristol
Michael J. Tresise, Southampton, Hants
G.H. Truran, Glastonbury, Somerset
John Usmar, Witheridge, Devon

David Wardrop, London SW6
R.M. Warwick, Northampton
Alan O. Watkins, Rainham, Gillingham, Kent
Mr John W. Watts, High Wycombe, Bucks
J.E. Webb, Tunbridge Wells, Kent
A.A. Webber, Taunton, Somerset
J.J. Webber, Minehead, Somerset
Mr John Weeks, Chedzoy, Bridgwater, Somerset
Andrew K. White, Lynton, Devon
C.A.P. White, Brompton Regis, Dulverton, Somerset
C.J. White
Sidney Whitehead, Sidmouth, Devon
R. Whitehouse, Borrowash, Derby
Mr V.A.G. Willins, Reigate, Surrey
Mr L.A. Wills, Exeter, Devon
Mrs Avice R. Wilson, New Brunswick, NJ, USA
Mr H.S. Withers, Witney, Oxon
Doreen and Ian Wood, Croydon, Surrey
Tony Woods, Minehead, Somerset
Dr A.R.H. Worssam, Porlock, Minehead, Somerset
K.J. Young, Harborne, Birmingham